This book is to be returned on or before

WITHDRAWN

PHEASANT SHOOTING

PHEASANT SHOOTING

CRAWFORD LITTLE

UNWIN

HYMAN

LONDON SYDNEY WELLINGTON

First published in Great Britain by Unwin Hyman, an imprint of Unwin
Hyman Limited, 1989

UNWIN HYMAN LIMITED
15/17 Broadwick Street, London W1V 1FP

Allen & Unwin Australia Pty Ltd
8 Napier Street, North Sydney, NSW 2060, Australia

Allen & Unwin New Zealand Ltd with the Port Nicholson Press
Compusales Building, 75 Ghuznee Street, Wellington, New Zealand

British Library Cataloguing in Publication Data

Little, Crawford
    Pheasant shooting.
1. Pheasants. Shooting
I. Title
799.2'48617
ISBN 0-04-440280-5

Typeset in 11½ on 14 point Times
Printed in Great Britain by Butler & Tanner Ltd, Frome and London

Contents

Glossary

Action connects barrels to stock and contains firing mechanism

Beavertail broad fore-end

Best gun product of a leading and skilful gunmaker

Boxlock most simple, rugged and cheap gun action

Brace two birds – not properly used to describe a bag of pheasants

Breech where cartridges are inserted into barrels of gun

Cast to bring the barrels in line with the shooter's eye the stock is set at a slight angle to that of the barrels

Cast-off the cast for a right-handed shooter, 'cast-on' for left-handed

Choke constriction at muzzle of barrels – concentrates the shot pattern and increases killing range (tightest constriction = full choke, no constriction = true cyclinder)

Covert a wood in which pheasants may be reared and released

Draw see 'Peg'

Drive when beaters chase the pheasants to fly over the guns

Ejector when the gun is opened at the breach, ejectors throw out the fired cartridge(s)

Fore-end wooden attachment beneath barrels to hold them in action

Forward allowance the lead allowed when shooting at moving targets – barrels must point ahead of the target when the gun is fired

Grace birds normally a cock and a hen pheasant gifted to each gun at the end of a shoot

Gun a gun is a weapon; a Gun is the individual using it

Load weight of shot contained in the cartridge

Mounting raising the gun to the shoulder

Multi-choke metal tubes inserted into muzzles of those guns made to accept them, giving a variety of choke options

Orders the host or organiser gives these at the start of the day – eg. are foxes or rabbits to be shot?

Over-and-under shotgun where two barrels are set one on top of the other

Pattern spread of shot

Peg position where gun stands – normally marked by a numbered wooden peg (see cover of this book). Guns will 'draw' for a number at start of day and normally move up two at each subsequent drive

Picker-up person with retrieving dogs to gather wounded and slain pheasants

Poult immature pheasant, not in mature plumage

Right-and-left where two birds are killed in quick succession, one by right, one by left barrel of a side-by-side

Rough shooting informal shooting, normally without beaters

Sewelling line long cord with ribbons or strips of plastic tied to it, strung across wood to encourage pheasants to gain height and speed before crossing guns

Self-opener when the top lever is pushed across, the barrels drop automatically, operating the ejectors and thus freeing a hand to grab two new cartridges. Aids fast reloading

Side-by-side shotgun with two barrels set alongside each other

Sidelock a more sophisticated action than the boxlock allowing for finer adjustments

Sight plane the shooter's view of the top of the barrels and rib as he aligns on the target

Sleeve or Slip 'sock' to protect the gun between drives

Stand where the team of guns stand during a drive or area from which birds are driven

Stock wooden part of gun, behind the action, that the shooter raises to his shoulder

Stop person placed to guard against pheasants making off on foot from a covert

Syndicate a team of paying guns, sharing the cost of their sport. May be resident on one shoot or travel to a number

Walking up when no beaters are employed, the guns will walk up and shoot at their own birds, often with close-hunting spaniels to flush the bird before them

1 A DAY ON THE PHEASANT SHOOT

November dawn rises slowly over a mellow countryside. The last leaves have fallen to reveal the intricacies of the woodland trees and hedgerows. The land steams in the early morning glow.

In the bareness of the wood, among the clumps of evergreens and cover, deep in the surviving warmth and shelter of Norway spruce, pheasants are coming awake. They shake the dew off their backs in a flurry of feathers and feel the first pangs of an empty stomach.

Two figures appear, both old worthies of the countryside. They have walked these fields as man and boy. Now that they have retired, they still like to make themselves useful. Five minutes later, they are standing on the pheasants' main exit routes from the wood, tapping their sticks gently to deter the breakfast-seeking birds that the old men can see scuttling about on the litter of leaves that carpet the woodland floor.

It is a big wood, perched high above a south-facing valley side. A long stretch of shelter belt, heading off to the west, forms the second leg of an L shape. The sun gives up its struggle to break through the filtered grey of the day. The old men, 'stops' as they are called, know that the keeper

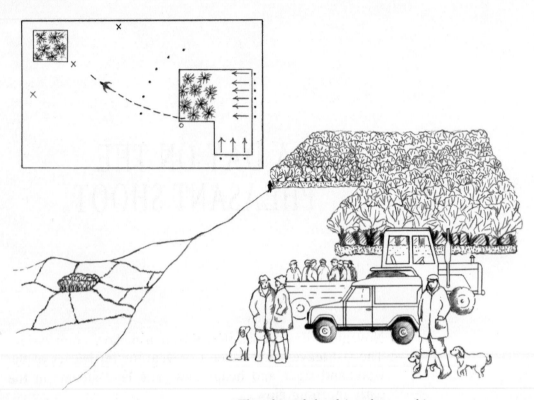

*The plan of the drive shows a big
wood, perched high above a south-facing
valley side with a long stretch of shelter
belt forming the second leg of an L shape.*

and host will be pleased. Pheasants hate to fly into a low
sun, and the Guns hate having to face it. Today it can be
ignored.

Two Land-Rovers and a tractor pulling a trailer laden
with men are coming up the farm track. They stop as
they get within fifty yards of the shelter belt. A keeper
opens the back door of one of the Land-Rovers and a
mixed pack of spaniels and labradors eagerly leap forth
and mill about while their masters clamber after them.
Soon three men, with eight dogs between them, break off
and make their way down towards the valley bottom. They
are the pickers-up and their job will be to place themselves

well behind the line of Guns to gather any wounded birds and then sweep forwards to make sure the Guns, after their own pick-up, have not missed any. With birds in the bag at £15 a head, besides any humanitarian considerations, they will have more than paid their way when they have picked two birds apiece. And on a big day they may find dozens that would otherwise have been missed.

One of the old stops at the lower end of the wood can see the beaters coming up to the end of the shelter belt. He can hear youthful voices raised, and quickly spots those who have not thought to don waterproof leggings. The stop sucks on his pipe and spits in a meditative way. 'Still, old Bert'll soon bring the young buggers to heel.'

Another convoy of vehicles has appeared, more luxurious than the last, a stream of Range Rovers and Volvo estate cars. Bringing up the rear is a battered old Ford Transit with Jimmy, the tractor driver, at the wheel. It will be his job to gather the birds, tie them in braces by the neck, and sling them on the racks in the back of the van. Instead of turning up the farm track, they drive into the field and park. Soon the vehicles are surrounded by men with guns, their ladies and their dogs. As the sounds of merry chatter drift up the valley, the old stop spits again. 'Aye, it's the boss as well as old Bert who'll have to bring some buggers to heel.' Game can hear and game can see, and cunning old pheasants are slinking back through the wood, searching for some way out. 'This is as good as being a fly on a farmhouse wall on the eve of Waterloo. Or seeing the Russian guns and the charging Light Brigade.' There is always the hint of military precision and organisation on any well-run shoot.

As the party of Guns and camp followers make their way along the valley floor, they fall out, one by one, as they reach each of the numbered pegs that the keeper set in the ground the previous day.

The keeper is waiting for the last Guns to get into position before he starts his men forwards. He has sent three beaters without dogs into the shelter belt, and he is keeping the other eight beaters with him, in a small group on the top side of the wood and keeping slightly behind those in the belt. The dogs are staying steadily at heel at this stage, and all is quiet except for the tap-tap-tap of the sticks in the belt, coaxing the pheasants to run, rather than fly, into the main wood.

Having reached the end of the belt, the keeper lines the rest of his team out along the wood. 'Stop when you're twenty yards short of the end, Tom. One of the stops is on the hedge and he will bring down the side,' he says.

'That's the last I'll see of them,' thinks the stop. 'I'm glad I came down to the bottom end of the wood and left Bill up at the top. Now, let's see what these Guns are up to. There's going to be some red faces when those birds come sailing out and turn down the valley.'

Indeed, this is the case. When the birds flush from the odd spots of cover dotted about in the wood, they soar out into the valley, then realise that there is no feature for them to fly towards. The nearest wood on the far side is down to the east, and so they turn towards this.

The effect, from below, is of birds flying hard to gain height, then setting their wings and dropping with a curl, accelerating off to the side. Some of the Guns have never experienced such testing birds and, indeed, there will be a few red faces at the end of the drive. But they cannot say that the birds were so high as to be out of range because, as the stop has noticed, one of their number has already plucked three or four down from the heavens, and the host has had a couple more.

Both men are killing their birds cleanly as they pass overhead, and both are doing it in a style that suggests that they have all the time in the world. Like all accomplished performers, they make it seem so easy. Neither of them is rushing in any way, belying any need for haste. One or two birds have slipped out low. All but one of the

Guns have ignored these. This one individual, knowing no better, is firing at these low, unsporting birds. No doubt the host or one of the other Guns will have a quiet word with him about only firing at the higher, more testing birds.

But the stop only spares a second to glance and swear at this youngster, still taking the occasional low bird that comes his way. As well as the first man to shine and the host, some of the other Guns are now getting their eye in, and making that little bit of extra effort to swing rapidly and accurately along the flight paths of birds passing overhead, squeezing off a shot as the barrels accelerate smoothly ahead of the bird's beak and really earning the glow of satisfaction when the pheasant's head flicks back and he tumbles down, clean killed. These birds, with a drop and a curl, are really testing the Guns to their limits.

'Still, not a bad team of Guns,' thinks the stop; 'not too bad at all.'

Half an hour later, the valley is quiet and empty, save for the Transit van, Jimmy the tractor driver and our friend the stop. They are chatting quietly, waiting for the picker-up who is making his way toward them. Jimmy leans out of the window.

'Come on then, boy. Room for a little one in the back. Let's be going. Guns moved on two minutes ago and we don't want to be missing all the fun. Bert says you're to get in behind Guns 2 and 3, back at the edge of the oak wood, but mind you don't send your dogs into the wood, because we'll be driving it after lunch.'

'All right, Grandpa,' says the picker-up, 'keep your hair on.' Then he jumps into the back with his dog. 'You got any baler twine, Grandpa? I've got another six for you here.'

'Good lad. You tie them up. Looks like it's going to be a good shoot today.'

The old stop sucks on his pipe, says 'Aye', and spits out of the window of the van, now speeding, rattling and bumping after the vehicles disappearing into the distance. 'Don't know many days that ain't.'

And nobody would give him an argument about that. No, old boy, not many days that ain't.

2 MODERN PHEASANT SHOOTING

Pheasants have been with us since the days of the Roman Empire. They were brought to Romano-British households as birds for the table, via the poultry yards of Italy, from Asia. The modern pheasant of today may be a mongrel as a result of interbreeding of the races, but its ancestry can be traced back to lands such as Mongolia, China and Japan.

In the way of things, pheasants escaped from captivity, and where a breeding pair came together in a congenial environment small pockets of wild populations began to grow. The Normans, in their inimitable way, soon after the conquest of 1066, were passing laws to protect them and issuing licences to kill them.

Rearing and Release

Pheasant numbers remained small and their distribution limited until the introduction of rearing and release for sport, which began in the late eighteenth century. It took another hundred years, encouraged by the introduction of the breech-loading shotgun with its vastly improved rate of fire compared to the muzzle-loader, coupled with the notorious appetites of shooting parties of the time, before

The cock pheasant.

Feeding young pheasants.

the art and science of rearing and release were honed to a high degree. By the end of the nineteenth century, it was no longer a case of how many pheasants could be reared but how many birds the estate, its woods and fields, could be squeezed to support.

Who Shoots?

This book is not intended as a social history of the last hundred years, so suffice it to say that the fortunes of the great landed estates which reached their zenith in the years leading up to the First World War have followed a downhill path since that time. In terms of pheasant shooting, however, this may not be such a bad thing. Certainly, now

9

that the wealth of the land is more evenly distributed far greater numbers are able to enjoy the sport than was ever possible in the past. Today only a handful of landowners are able to run their shoots as totally private affairs. Of the rest, the keenest will probably be involved in what might be called a 'hidden' syndicate. Their 'guests' are the owners of neighbouring estates and shoots, invited in the sure knowledge and on the clear understanding that the invitation will be reciprocated. The ten days of sport for the host and seven guest Guns may not be the lavish affairs of grandfather's day, but with return matches the estate owner can expect ten days on his own land and seventy more on that of his guests. For many, this will be too much, and half the days can be let off through a sporting agency to a visiting team of Guns, which will bring in some income to meet costs yet still leave the estate owner with two or three days shooting a week throughout the three main months of the pheasant-shooting season, from the leaves falling in November through to the last of the 'cocks only' days at the end of January.

There are many estate owners, however, who have neither the time nor the inclination to shoot on this scale. They may form a syndicate of paying Guns, possibly getting two 'free' Guns in return for the land and some feed, so that they can invite a guest each day. Or, of course, there are landowners who have no interest at all in shooting, and then the ground may be let off to a syndicate which takes full responsibility for the shoot.

The Costs

The responsibilities of a shoot are as hard on the syndicate members' pockets as they are on their organisational abilities. As soon as a full-time keeper is employed, the costs begin to soar. How are they made up?

Based on Game Conservancy figures which were published more than a decade ago, but which I have adjusted for the purposes of simplifying the illustration, the figures may be as follows, as a percentage of the total costs.

	per cent
Keeper	30
Rearing	20
Transport	10
Rent and rates	20
Covert feeding	10
Other costs	10
	100

Therefore, on a shoot where the keeper is rearing 3,000 birds, fairly typical costs might be as follows:

Keeper	£9,000
Rearing	£6,000
Transport	£3,000
Rent and rates	£6,000
Covert feeding	£3,000
Other costs	£3,000
Total	£30,000
Per bird reared	£10

However, before anybody imagines that they can expect to shoot 3,000 birds from 3,000 reared, it must be recognised that probably fewer than half of these will be actually recovered. Therefore, if the wild stock is there to swell the bag, such a shoot could expect to shoot an average of about 150 birds over ten days. With 1,500 birds accounted for at season's close, the cost will have been £20 per bird.

The Search for Economies

This represents expensive sport. Each day is costing £3,000 – or close to £400 for each individual in a team of eight

11

guns. Some of them are going to look hard at ways of maximising the output from the fixed costs of keeper, transport, rent and rates and some of the other costs. If the keeper is pushed a bit harder, he may be able to rear and release 4,000 birds, regarded as the maximum for a single-handed man. This might bring the costs down to about £17 per bird. However, it also means that while they are getting more birds at a smaller cost per head they are, at the end of the day, spending more. They could introduce more Guns to the shoot, but they may already feel that the line is cramped with eight Guns. The alternative is that they let off a day.

However, as soon as this option is considered some bright spark is going to notice that at the going rate, which seldom exceeds £15 per bird on commercial let days, there is a still cheaper alternative.

Commercial Shoots

The reasons why some commercial shoots are able to offer pheasant shooting at what is apparently less than cost would require a fairly lengthy and involved consideration, but at the end of the day they rely heavily on maximising the use of fixed costs and economies of scale, in much the same way that large supermarket chains are able to under-cut the smaller grocer. For those who find no satisfaction in running a shoot of their own and whose interest starts and ends with the day's shooting, taking one or a number of let days becomes a very attractive proposition.

Today there are a growing number of what have come to be called 'travelling syndicates'. They are seen in all shapes and forms. Often their foundation is a small shoot on which no keeper is employed, certainly not on a full-time basis. Through their own do-it-yourself and self-help efforts, they are able to enjoy some pheasant and rough shooting at minimal cost. And then they use the rest of their budgets to take days where and when they want: maximum enjoyment for minimum cost and responsibility.

The recognition of a day's pheasant shooting as a near-perfect form of business entertaining has further enhanced and encouraged the growth of these commercial shoots, as well as the numbers of sporting agencies which act as 'introducer' between shoots and prospective guests. On some shoots, the production of the total package of exactly the form of day required, down to the last bird and final drop of champagne, has been perfected.

The Future

In the coming years, ignoring the aspirations of a vitriolic minority who would see an impotent countryside denuded of its essential character, pheasant shooting is likely to experience a steady acceleration down the path which it has already been following for years. Basically, this will be a loss of the middle ground – those shoots where the costs of a full-time keeper are becoming harder to justify. I think that the trend will continue towards, at one end of the scale, those self-help shoots, possibly with a part-time keeper, where the members are able to put in time and effort in place of hard cash. At the other end, big shoots will concentrate more and more on financial efficiency and attracting the business entertainers and travelling syndicates.

There was an unhappy trend, when business entertaining emerged as a potent force on the shooting scene, for the accent to be on quantity rather than quality. Probably, when they started, the captains of industry did not know what they should expect. Equally, shoot organisers realised that the purpose of the day was not to embarrass important clients by producing birds that flew so high and so fast as to be completely beyond the Guns' capabilities. However, with the passing years and as experience grew, the men of business wanted more testing sport, and the men who organised it for them realised that now these men were maturing into good shots they were well up to the challenge.

The man who had not come to shooting until middle age, and then only because he had been invited by a business contact, discovered that he really enjoyed his day and, by the following season, was making sure that he had regular shooting. And so business entertaining, while criticised by the more traditional camps, has in reality led to an influx of both shooting men and hard cash at a time when without them the shooting scene might have been forced towards unattractive but necessary changes.

Today, with the minimum of exceptions, the talk is all of quality rather than quantity. Even the most hard-bitten of commercial shoot organisers realises that if he shows poor birds the Guns will not return. Shooting parties have shown, time and again, that they are willing to pay a premium price for quality pheasants sweeping high above the line of Guns. They would far rather shoot 50 scorchers that tested them to their limits than 200 of which not one was memorable.

Surely it is with economies of production and this concentration of thinking on quality rather than quantity that the future of pheasant shooting must be found.

3 CHOOSING A GUN

The vast majority of those choosing their first gun for game shooting will finally decide upon a double-barrelled hammerless gun. As is often said, the experience of generations of sportsmen has shown this to be the ideal choice. Equally, that experience has highlighted the 12-bore as the most appropriate calibre of gun.

` In recent times the traditional place of honour enjoyed by this standard gun has been questioned in the sporting press. At one level, this could be described as little more than writers searching about for something new to talk about. However, there is a great deal more to it than that and, if only to affirm the very real benefits of the side-by-side 12-bore, some time should be spent in at least considering the alternatives before delving into the various forms and possibilities offered in the traditional gun.

Side-by-Side or Over-and-Under

Until fairly recently it was rare to see an over-and-under gun on a game shoot, but that situation has changed very rapidly. The reason is plain to see. Clay-pigeon shooting is now a very popular sport. For this type of shooting, the over-and-under reigns supreme. For the growing number of shooters who come to game shooting via the clay-pigeon circuit, the narrow sight plane, pointability and feel of an over-and-under have become totally familiar.

Familiarity with a gun is fundamental to successful shooting. When these clay-pigeon shooters try to make the change to a side-by-side, because it is not familiar to them they find that their performance suffers. Probably, if they made a real effort to familiarise themselves with the side-by-side when it came time to shoot clays again, they would then have lost something of the feel for the over-and-under and their scores would suffer accordingly. It is a case of swings and roundabouts and they feel they lose either way. They decide that the over-and-under is the gun for them and, as they are expected to spend a large amount of money to be a member of a syndicate shoot, they do not see why they should change to a side-by-side. The attitude could be summed up as 'he who pays the piper calls the tune' – and fair enough.

On the other hand, there are still a very large number of shoots where the side-by-side is considered the correct and proper choice and the over-and-under is regarded as little better than a repeater. Such shoots represent the majority in areas where clay-pigeon shooting has never really caught on, and even where it has there are shoots where many if not all of the members and guests will consider clay-pigeons as nothing more than practice for game shooting. A man wishing to join such a shoot will not be considered favourably if it is discovered that he intends to use an over-and-under, certainly not if the organiser can make up his numbers from those who prefer a side-by-side. And a guest to such a shoot who uses an over-and-under, unless he is an exceptionally close friend or valuable contact, is running the very real risk of not being invited back.

The reason for this prejudice against the over-and-under on many shoots is, sometimes, nothing more than a respect for tradition. However, it can go a great deal deeper and be

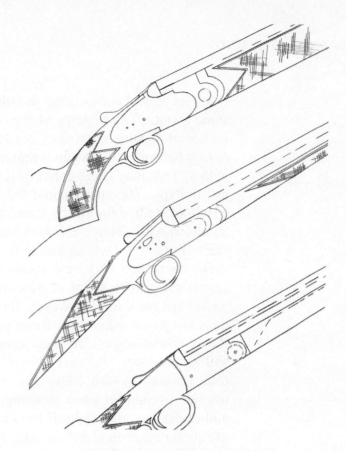

*Gun types (from the top): sidelock
over-and-under, sidelock side-by-side, and
boxlock.*

tied up with the spirit of amateurism in sport. On a game
shoot – be it concerned with pheasant, grouse, partridges,
duck, woodcock, snipe or whatever – there is no place for a
competitive attitude, certainly not on the surface. Nobody
would ever think to mention that they visit a shooting
school to get in some practice, and the jealously greedy
competitive Shot who seems most concerned with bagging
more than his share, and worries about how many birds
he has shot for however many cartridges, is considered
as undesirable as a dangerous Shot who might give his
companions a broadside.

Being aware of this attitude, it seems far easier to explain
why the over-and-under, being so closely associated with

17

clay-pigeon and competitive shooting, is not acceptable on some shoots. The motives of the over-and-under user are immediately suspect. It does not help if he insists that his reason for using such a gun is that he shoots so much better with it. That may suggest that he is probably a competitive, greedy type. This rubs against the grain of men who adopt a style of studied indifference and who have been raised in a culture which states it is how you play the game rather than whether you win or lose that is important.

So, there are very real social reasons for those who expect or wish to shoot in 'side-by-side company' not to go against tradition. However, there is another, obvious, question to be asked: are there really any advantages in the over-and-under? In fact, many knowledgeable men will assert that, all other things being equal, assuming total familiarity with either gun, the advantages lie with the side-by-side for game shooting. The fact that the over-and-under has proved itself the most suitable weapon for use in clay-pigeon shooting does not mean that it is best for *all* forms of shooting. 'Horses for courses' – and it is important to recognise the very real differences between clay-pigeon and game shooting.

When shooting clay-pigeons, the sportsman can go to the first stand and study the flight of the clays as others shoot at them. There will be no surprises. The clays will continue to fly at exactly the same speed and on the same line. When the sportsman's turn to shoot comes, besides knowing the exact details of the clay's flight he can settle himself into a state of readiness and the clay will not be thrown until he calls 'pull'. Clay-pigeon shooting calls for a carefully studied and almost mechanical approach.

In contrast, the sportsman shooting live quarry is never really sure of the where, when and how of the next target. On the driven pheasant shoot, a variety of medium-high birds overhead and to left and right may be interrupted by a really high bird, or one curling across the line of the Guns, possibly followed by a woodcock flitting along the canopy of the wood, and then a long, crossing shot at a bird that a neighbouring Gun has hit but failed to kill cleanly. All other things being equal, the side-by-side, being normally lighter, better balanced and faster handling, is the more adaptable weapon.

There is another point in favour of the side-by-side, and it concerns the speed of reloading and thus the rate of fire. This is particularly important when shooting driven game. Even on those shoots that have no interest in showing a quantity of birds, where there is no desire to show a continuous stream of driven pheasants, many birds will flush in twos, threes or small bouquets. Birds will run on ahead of the line of beaters and take cover in, say, a patch of brambles. When the beaters work up to it, their steady tapping might push out two birds, then one more five seconds later, then three more in fairly quick succession. Rate of fire can be very important to the sportsman facing such a flush of birds.

In fact, besides safety aspects in a gun that does not drop open at the breech to be unloaded quickly, and to be seen to be unloaded, this is one reason why repeating guns – automatics and pumps – never caught on in this country, except for clay shooting, vermin control, wildfowling and other situations where rate of fire is not particularly important. True, the repeater can fire a short burst quickly, but then it has to be reloaded, which is a laborious operation. With a double-barrelled gun, reloading fairly quickly, you might get off eight or ten shots in a minute – far more than with a repeater – and as the time extends so the difference in fire power of a double-barrelled gun over a repeater grows wider and wider.

Now, it may not be immediately apparent, but the over-and-under has to be opened and closed through a much greater arc than a side-by-side, in order to clear the lower barrel from the breech; even then many sportsmen find the lower barrel rather inaccessible for really slick reloading. This does not matter at all in clay-pigeon shooting, where the target is not presented until it is called for and as much time as necessary can be taken to reload, but it can be very frustrating in the face of a prolonged stream of birds.

Finally, to the eyes of most game shooters, the side-by-side has more elegant lines and feels more pleasant in the hand. Obviously, this is a personal matter, but it is not unimportant. If a man feels that a gun looks and feels right, the weapon will instil in him the confidence to shoot to his full potential, far better than he would with a gun that he felt was clumsy and looked all wrong and out of place. The theme that the looks of a gun are fundamentally important to most shooting men will be developed throughout this chapter. Such matters as the figure of the timber used for the stock and the quality of engraving on the action faces do nothing to improve the gun's performance in purely mechanical terms but, for some, they serve to boost morale and therefore should not be ignored. As stated, this is a personal matter and there are many men who prefer the looks and feel of an over-and-under.

To summarise, if a sportsman has become familiar with the over-and-under during an early career of clay-pigeon shooting and finds that he cannot take to a side-by-side and does not expect to be a regular guest at shoots where tradition rules, then there is no reason why he should not stick to his chosen weapon. However, besides the social considerations of those who expect to be invited here and there, there are some very real practical reasons for starting off with, and becoming familiar with, the side-by-side. It is a gun for all seasons and reasons, a weapon that can be taken anywhere, in any company.

Case for the Over-and-Under

If all this sounds dismissive of the over-and-under gun, it is meant rather as a guide to choosing a first gun for game shooting, and an explanation of some of the social prejudices that may be encountered. Despite all the arguments in favour of the side-by-side for game shooting, there is a case to be made in favour of the over-and-under, particularly for pheasants. However, because I feel the side-by-side will long remain the principal weapon for live rather than inanimate shooting, a fuller discussion of the over-and-under has been left to the end of this chapter.

Boxlock or Sidelock

With any double-barrelled gun, there are two main actions to choose between in the modern hammerless form. These are the sidelock and the boxlock.

Traditionally, the sidelock has always been the more expensive of the two actions. Well-heeled sportsmen look no further than for a sidelock produced by one of the famous London firms of gunmakers.

The boxlock, on the other hand, was less expensive to produce to a comparable standard, and came to be regarded as a suitable weapon for sporting farmers, parsons, junior officers, rough shooters and wildfowlers. Equally, because the boxlock was accepted as the most robust action of the two and far easier to maintain, it became the favoured weapon for the colonies, when such things still existed. Gunmakers with the skill and experience to work on a finely tuned sidelock action were thin on the ground up the Khyber Pass, among the snipe marshes of Malaya and on the game-bearing plains of southern Africa.

Market forces came to bear. At a time when, and to men to whom, price was immaterial, the best sidelock was found to be superior to the best boxlock, the main arguments in favour of the best sidelock being its finer balance and superior trigger pulls. Edwardian gentlemen who shot day after day, season after season, and fired as many cartridges in one year as their modern counterparts might hardly expect to use in a lifetime, could have their shooting ruined by an ill-balanced gun, by which they meant anything less than perfect, or a slight variation in the pressure required on the trigger to cause the hammer to fall and detonate the cartridge.

To those shooting men who were able to afford the very best, and for whom only the very best would do, the best had to be the sidelock. It was the thoroughbred gun, while the boxlock came to be regarded as the cart-horse, perfectly suitable for certain tasks but not for driven game on the great shoots.

Having recognised and fostered the appeal of the sidelock to the upper, expensive, end of the market, it was natural that the gun trade should lavish their best care, attention and expertise on producing such guns. So it is that, in the way of things, the best materials and the greatest time and effort have gone into producing the best guns, the very best of which will be sidelocks. From selecting the timber for the stock and fore-end, through the finishing of the barrels, and the precision of the internal parts of the action, down to the intricate engraving of the tiniest screw-head, make no mistake, no effort or cost is spared in producing guns in this class. But it is not just the appearance of such guns that sets them apart. It is as if the team of craftsmen involved in making the gun have gifted it with a life and soul. In the hand, it is an extension of its user, coming up to the shoulder in a way that makes a poor-quality gun feel like nothing more than a fencepost with a couple of water pipes lashed to it. Of course, just as it takes a fine musician to bring out the very best in a Stradivarius, rather than simply a 'good' violin, so it takes a top-notch performer to make the most of a best gun. But that is not to say that a top-quality sidelock is not a joy to use for any man.

Further down the social and price range came a cut-off point where for the same money the gunmaker could offer his customer a very basic sidelock without the frills or a top-quality boxlock. Technical logic and common sense dictated that it was far more sensible to have a good boxlock rather than a poor sidelock but, still, those market forces were playing their part.

We now come back to the theme of sportsmen choosing the weapon in which they have most confidence – the gun that looks and feels the best. The shooting world recognised that the great men all used sidelocks and, therefore, others felt that they would be able to shoot so much better themselves if they could only have a similar gun. It did not matter if one was the best quality and the other the standard; they were both sidelocks. It was this attitude which killed the market for best quality boxlocks, with a few notable exceptions. And thus the standing of the sidelock as the thoroughbred and the boxlock as the cart-horse was enhanced and confirmed. For a given middle-of-the-range price, it should be possible to obtain a better boxlock than a sidelock, but, since the demand for such guns is so small because of their lack of customer appeal, the supply is very limited. Most men when shooting game, given the choice, prefer to shoot with a sidelock, so that is the gun that the trade produces.

The clean, elegant lines of the sidelock action have greater appeal to most eyes than the square, rather solid looks of the boxlock. People have shown, over the years, that they are prepared to pay a great deal for it. That appeal, even to those who lack the practice to make the most of a best gun's finer balance and take full advantage of its crisp, clean and carefully regulated trigger pulls, continues as a theme throughout the following considerations of whether to choose English or foreign, new or second-hand.

English or Foreign

The situation that existed for generations of shooting men has now been described. At the top end of the market, those who could afford them would choose a best sidelock.

In the middle of the range, there was a choice between best boxlocks and standard sidelocks and, due to the inherent appeals of the thoroughbred gun, the sidelock remained the first choice. Below that, the boxlock was the only choice.

Then everything changed. What had been little more than a trickle of guns into the British market from Continental Europe became a flood. The Spanish gun trade, more than any other, set out to catch the middle and lower end of the market. By various means, the Spaniards were able to produce sidelocks not just at lower prices than their English counterparts, not only lower than a new English boxlock, but comparable in price to a second-hand boxlock of advanced years and tarnished appearance, if not reputation.

Of course, these Spanish guns could not be seriously compared to English sidelocks but, to the eyes of the average shooting man, they looked very similar, if not quite identical, and they quickly caught on. The message came through both loud and clear – closest to the English ideal and at an affordable price.

It happened again. Now that sidelocks were being offered at a comparable price, many sportsmen were quick to confirm afresh that, given the choice, they would prefer to shoot with a sidelock rather than a boxlock.

Something else was happening which served to enhance the position of the relatively cheaper imported gun. The English gun developed a reputation as an investment over and above its functional use. Collectors, rather than users, sought them out avidly. Of course, an investment realises nothing until it is cashed in and many users of English guns were tempted into selling and replacing them with a Spanish counterpart. Others, on seeing the escalating prices of what they had – and particularly if they mixed their driven shooting with some informal rough days and wildfowling – decided that their guns were too valuable to be taken into the field, except on high days and holidays.

Both classes of gun users were looking for replacements, either full- or part-time, for their valuable English guns. They sought out the 'closest to the English ideal' at a fraction of the price. And, because such guns as the AYA range (Aguirre y Aranzabal) could be ordered to individual specification, allowing the purchaser, within limits, to choose a gun that was very close to his original in such matters as weight and barrel length, stock length, and so on, there was little hesitation. The imported gun might not be of the same high quality as the gun that it was replacing, but near enough, for all practical purposes, as to make no noticeable difference in performance.

It wasn't every man who was pleased with his Spanish sidelock. Unfortunately, one or two rogues jumped on the Spanish bandwagon. On the surface, their guns may carry a thin veneer of respectability but, in the hand and on closer inspection, they look more like the product of the local blacksmith and plumber than of a gunsmith. However, experience grew and lessons were learned. Such established firms as AYA and those gunmakers producing guns for Gunmark have earned both trust and respect, while others fall by the wayside.

New or Second-Hand

It may seem an apparently outrageous statement, but many sportsmen will say that even if they could afford a new English gun, if they were so rich that the price simply did not matter, they would still look to the second-hand market. This isn't a dig at modern gunmakers but rather recognition of the fact that, in their opinion, the English gun reached its zenith in the years between the two world wars.

There are even some who, with their hearts set on an English gun but wishing it to be made to their specification, would search out a between-the-wars gun which retains a good, serviceable action, but whose barrels and stock have been neglected or are worn out. The barrels and stock they would throw away, but the action would be taken to its original maker with a request for new barrels and stock to the person's specific requirements. Barrels come and stocks go, but some of the actions, produced with such great skill and patience by a generation of craftsmen no longer with us, seem to go on for ever.

For those with little knowledge of guns, those who cannot spot some of the back-street tricks to cover faults in a gun, the best course of action when seeking a second-hand weapon is to go to a man with a reputation to lose, possibly the original maker, who is prepared to offer some sort of satisfactory guarantee. If you have a knowledgeable friend who is prepared to come with you and inspect the gun as well, that is better still.

If you are buying from a private individual, or a man whose reputation is not completely established, it would be unwise to hand over payment until the gun has been thoroughly checked and given the all-clear by a reputable gunsmith. In the case of a gun which requires some work to bring it up to standard, he will be able to provide an estimate of the cost, and it can then be decided whether or not the gun is worth buying, and at what price.

The situation is slightly different with Spanish guns. Most prospective purchasers will, because of their relatively low price, be considering a new gun. However, as the history of Spanish guns in this country continues to grow, as more and more of the original purchasers die off or retire from shooting, the second-hand trade in these guns is bound to become more active.

A number of these guns, possibly those bought by the owners of best English guns for the less formal occasions, may have seen very hard use and inadequate maintenance. Human nature being what it is, the less expensive gun may not have received the same level of care as its more valuable counterparts.

Equally, many of these guns have been bought by 'occasional' shooters, men who rely heavily on invitations and may only shoot a few boxes of cartridges in a season. Such a gun, if carefully maintained, might represent really excellent value for money. Whatever the case, the same rules of seeking a man with a reputation, guarantees, or qualified independent advice, still apply.

Supremacy of the 12-bore

For the uninitiated, it has to be explained that shotguns come in a fairly extensive range of sizes. The bigger the gun, all other things being equal, the heavier the charge of shot that it will fire. In practical terms, the biggest gun that can be fired from the shoulder is a 4-bore, a truly mighty weapon that can throw up to 4 oz of large shot. If such a gun still has a place in the shooting scene, it is when geese are pursued below the sea wall.

The 4-bore represents the extreme of the goose and duck shooter's heavy armour which includes 8-bores, 10-bores and, most popular of all, the magnum 12-bore. These are all guns designed to kill at the very extremes of range, up to 60 and even 70 yards.

At the other end of the scale there is the 28-bore and the ·410, but, because they are able to throw only a light charge of shot, their effective range is limited to about 20 yards, and so they are regarded as suitable only as a first gun for a boy.

In between the little and large of the gunmaker's products, there is the standard 12-bore, the 16-bore and the 20-bore. Any of these might be considered as suitable for most game-shooting purposes.

Incidentally, for the inquiring mind, the designation of the various calibres goes back to the early days of shooting and the use of muzzle loaders. If 1 lb of lead was melted down and made into four identical spherical balls, these balls would fit the muzzle of a 4-bore. If the lead was made into twenty balls, they would fit the barrel of a 20-bore, and so on. The only exception is the ·410, which is a linear measure – 0·410 of an inch – of the internal diameter of the gun's barrel.

To return to the original point, if you fire a heavy load of shot out of a light gun, recoil will be excessive and, therefore, those big wildfowling guns had to be made very heavy. However, this obviously meant that they were tiring, unwieldy weapons. The handling qualities of the gun were sacrificed in order to extend its range by increasing its weight and thus allowing it to fire as heavy a load of large shot as possible, large shot being able to kill at far greater range than small shot.

A general formula was evolved that, certainly where a number of shots would have to be fired, the gun should weigh 96 times the weight of the shot charge. That seems an odd number – why not 100 times the weight? The answer, of course, is that it means a 6 lb gun can comfortably fire a 1 oz load of shot.

Shot loads and cartridges are considered in detail in Chapter 4. For now it is enough to know that long experience has shown that a shot load of from 1 to 1⅛ oz of shot is ideal for game shooting at normal ranges. This implies guns with a weight of from 6 to 6¾ lb – not too heavy for a good, fast handling game gun. Such a shot load and gun weight represent the ideal compromise for game shooting. With a lighter load of shot range is reduced, and with a heavier gun ease of handling is lost. Today nothing has changed since the time when the 12-bore established its supremacy as the ideal game gun, a weapon designed to kill at up to 50 yards in the right hands.

Gun Weight and Barrel Length

Whilst gun weight is largely a function of barrel length, I have already noted that one of the advantages of the side-by-side is that, all other things being equal, it is usually lighter than a comparable over-and-under. A long-barrelled side-by-side of 6¾ lb would be regarded as a 'heavy' whereas an over-and-under of the same weight would be regarded as a lightweight. Equally, a side-by-side with 28-inch barrels may weigh less than an over-and-under with 26-inch barrels. However, as we have to have some basis to work from, let us consider the case of side-by-side guns in 12-bore and make the following our starting-point.

A *lightweight gun* is one with 25- or 26-inch barrels, weighing up to 6¼ lb.

A *medium gun* is one with 27- or 28-inch barrels, weighing from 6¼ to 6¾ lb.

A *heavy gun* is one with 29- or 30-inch barrels, weighing in excess of 6¾ lb.

Lightweight guns with their short barrels were a development of the earlier part of this century. The reasoning behind them is that they reduce fatigue and that they are a quicker-handling weapon, particularly useful to the driven-game shooter. In the past, when birds had been shot by walking up or over dogs, and often at extremes of range, a heavy charge of fairly large shot proved ideal, and it was necessary to have a heavy gun to absorb the recoil associated with such a load. But now that driven shooting was the thing, largely conducted at closer range and at birds which exposed their vital organs to the charge of shot rather than flying away to be shot up the rear end, lighter loads were all that was necessary. As shooting with a pair of guns and employing a loader became a more widespread practice, the fast-handling lightweight gun seemed a definite advantage for both quicker and improved shooting.

Robert Churchill was the man to popularise the 25-inch barrels and he said at the time that he regarded them as the most significant contribution that he had been able to make to the improvement of the sporting gun in his time. Indeed, some would say that it was the *only*

*Robert Churchill was the man to
popularise the 25-inch barrels.*

significant contribution made to the sporting gun in this century.

Churchill regarded 30-inch barrels as relics of a past age which gave no advantages in terms of ballistics or killing power, and maintained that the advantages of his 25-inch gun were a decrease in weight and an improvement in balance and ease of handling. He made some fairly extravagant claims for his guns: 'The many years of my life that I have devoted to giving instruction have clearly shown that it takes approximately four times as much ammunition and four times as many hours of practice to enable the average individual to attain a modern standard of efficiency with the long barrel as to reach the same stage with the twenty-five-inch barrelled gun.'

These words are taken from his book *Game Shooting*. Warming to his theme, he goes on: 'Just as we now find it more convenient to live in smaller houses, and use lighter and shorter fishing rods, so in the matter of guns, the most convenient gun is the modern lightweight twenty-five inch.'

What follows hints at a strong reaction to the derision he received at the hands of the devotees of longer barrels when he sought to popularise his guns in the years following the First World War: 'My short-barrelled guns are not a wedding of old and new, they are something quite new altogether. I claim for them that they handle like a 20-bore, shoot as hard as a 10-bore, look as long as thirty inches when aligned on a bird and, most important of all, that they quicken the faculties of the shooter and reduce fatigue because they are twice as comfortable as the old heavy guns to carry.'

Well now, the first part of that, about 20-bores and 10-bores, might be excusable as a piece of advertising propaganda for his own products, something akin to describing a family saloon as having the same handling qualities as a sports car, and with a load space equal to an articulated lorry, but that's about as far as it goes. A pity, really, because it takes something away from the rest of what he had to say.

There is absolutely no doubt that the shorter, lighter gun is the quickest-handling of all. But there are one or two things to be understood on this point. First, Churchill was a short, stocky man and, on the whole, short and stocky men require weapons in similar vein, while tall men do best with longer barrels. Both are in proportion. Second, when Churchill talks about the savings in time and cartridges involved in enabling an average individual to attain a 'modern standard of efficiency', he would be teaching them his own fairly original style, which depended, more than any other method perhaps, on a perfectly fitted gun and is, if anything, a form of snap shooting.

This shooting style is important. Many shooting men found that they could not take to it, certainly not for pheasants. Remember that Churchill was shooting and writing through a time when the partridge was still a very essential ingredient of the sportsman's year. Taking a right-and-left out of a covey of the little brown bird as the covey explodes like shrapnel over a hedge or belt of trees, right on top of the Guns, and shooting driven grouse as they hurtle down the contours of a moor, is a very different proposition from taking the high driven pheasant. Partridge and grouse require a fast shooting style and inspire a quick punchy swing. With the regal steady approach of a high-flying pheasant it is so very easy to fail to swing sufficiently and end up poking at the bird. If you like, partridge and grouse are shot in quickstep time, while pheasants are shot at the pace of an old-time waltz. An error of a couple of inches on a close partridge will be magnified to as many yards at a long-range pheasant.

In their book *The Shot Gun*, T. D. S. Purdey and Captain J. A. Purdey found a rather nice way of describing the merits and otherwise of short and long barrels. They said that if you raise a walking stick to a mark it will come on very quickly but that it is then hard to hold it on the mark because it is unsteady. Then, if you point a long fishing rod at the same mark, it is harder to get it on but, once there, it is relatively easier to hold it steady.

The same is just as true of short and long barrels. The very short are fast-handling at one extreme and at the other extreme long, 30-inch barrels are slow-handling but steady.

Much will depend upon the individual. A short, stocky man might find that he does rather better with 25-inch, while a tall man, taller than six foot, will be able to use 29- and 30-inch barrels to full potential on really high birds. A man of average height and build will find the ideal compromise between fast and steady handling in a gun with 27- or 28-inch barrels, a gun that weighs within an ounce or two of 6½ lb and which will handle cartridges of 1 and 1 1⁄16 oz perfectly, with an occasional 1⅛ oz if he feels it really necessary.

What a long and tortured trail to confirming that most men will be best suited with a medium-weight medium-barrel-length 12-bore modern game gun! However, if this rather long-winded discussion has done something to ensure your confidence in the popular choice, it will have been well worth while. As has been said, confidence is the bedrock of successful shooting and, if the gun is suspect, its user will not be able to shoot to his full potential.

An Over-and-Under for Pheasants

The social and other considerations used as arguments in favour of the traditional side-by-side 12-bore game gun have been set out at the start of this chapter. In many ways, it is the social arguments that still weigh heaviest against the over-and-under. Personally, I can see no logical argument against a man wishing to use such a gun. Any gun that can be opened at the breech is just as safe, or potentially dangerous, as any other. And if a man finds he performs better with an over-and-under, well, do we not all seek to acquire a gun with which we will be able to perform to our maximum potential? And, for some of us, particularly those who come to game shooting via clay-pigeon shooting, and the many game shots who in fact spend more time in shooting clays, because of familiarity that gun will be an over-and-under.

On this score of familiarity, many will choose a gun for game shooting that is as close as possible to their competition over-and-under in terms of weight, handling and balance. This will always be so, but there is another course of action which avoids the very real criticism that the standard over-and-under 12-bore is a bit too heavy and slow-handling for driven shooting. It is not for nothing that recent years have seen an explosion in the number of 20-bores offered with the over-and-under configuration. Many of these guns, with their 28- and even 30-inch barrels, seem to be purpose-built for plucking high pheasants down from the heavens. They are becoming ever more popular. What, if any, are the advantages of an over-and-under specifically in regard to high pheasants, and what, if any, are the disadvantages in going down from a 12- to a 20-bore in order to reduce weight to a handy level?

Advantages of an Over-and-Under

A shotgun is pointed, rather than aimed. Accurate pointing is a product of two things: manual and visual pointability. Now, in terms of manual pointability, there is nothing to beat a finely balanced 'best' English sidelock side-by-side, fitted to the individual user. It comes up like an extension of the left index finger. Only top-quality sidelock over-and-unders could run in the same race, in my opinion, and only a handful could push for a close second, with one or two of them managing a nose-to-nose finish.

Side-by-sides, however, for all that can be said in their favour in terms of manual pointability, tend to be lacking when it comes to visual pointability. This has little effect when shooting birds at medium range, particularly with a gun that throws fairly open patterns, but a small error at short range is multiplied many times at extreme range.

Sight down the barrels of a side-by-side with the standard plain, slightly dished top rib, and what you see is a rather vague amalgamation of indistinct barrels and the shadows at either side of the rib, with a distinct sense of breadth. In fact, a really high pheasant is likely to occupy little more than a quarter of the total muzzle breadth.

Now look down an over-and-under and all that you see is the flat file-cut or knurled rib stretching out, thin and precise, straight onto the target. Even the highest pheasant is not overlapped, and it is immediately clear whether the swing is spot on line of flight or slightly off to either side.

Equally, and most important, those who are used to shooting with an over-and-under are totally familiar with this sighting plane which, with care not to create a 'poky' aiming style, can be used to make fine adjustments, particularly on those long-range shots.

Let's be honest, aiming is an ever-present possibility with an over-and-under, and this is the reason why they are seldom fitted to the individual. If they were, I believe they could start to realise their full potential. However, a neat fit is not so important for clay shooters who know exactly where their next clay is coming from and going to as it is for the man who is faced with a stream of shots where no two are the same and where there may be little, if any, time to adapt to each one.

However, of all game birds, the driven pheasant is probably the most predictable and gives plenty of time for the shooter to study its flight and succeed in spite of his ill-fitting gun.

The 20-bore Over-and-Under

Many men can shoot pheasants happily with a 12-bore over-and-under weighing in excess of 7 lb, for the very same reasons that they can use an ill-fitting gun, certainly on average driven pheasants. However, if they changed to a rather lighter gun, knocking 1 lb off the overall weight, they could do even better. In terms of over-and-unders, this leads us towards the 20-bore.

The problem is that the 20-bore cartridge contains a lighter load of shot than a 12-bore. How much of a disadvantage does this involve?

Many men who shoot pheasants with a 12-bore are happy to use true cylinder barrels and 1 oz loads. The standard 20-bore cartridge contains $^{13}\!/_{16}$ oz of shot. Obviously, in order to achieve the same effective range the pattern has to be tightened up slightly and this is done with the introduction of choke at the gun muzzle. This is described in some detail in the next chapter.

Comparing the 1 oz load from a true cylinder with the $^{13}\!/_{16}$ oz load from an improved cylinder, using No. 7 shot, we find from tables of exact pellet density in a 30-inch circle at 40 yards 136 and 138 respectively – identical for all practical purposes.

I have yet to hear a man say, 'If only I had my gun bored true rather than improved cylinder, I would have hit that bird.'

Over and above these open patterns, the standard 20-bore load does not score so well. For example, the 20-bore would need a half choke to throw a pattern equivalent in density to a 1 oz load from an improved cylinder barrel.

However, tight chokes are associated only with the most testing of pheasants, and an interesting fact can now be introduced. This is not the place to go into the whys and wherefores but one of the reasons that the $^{13}\!/_{16}$ oz load is the standard for 20-bores, just as the 1 or $1^{1}\!/_{16}$ oz load is the standard for 12-bores, is that, as you increase the shot load and effectively lengthen the shot column, pattern quality will deteriorate, becoming patchy and probably less effective than the lighter load. However, and most important, this can be cured with the introduction of a fairly high degree of choke.

The over-and-under 20-bore, so long as it weighs in excess of 6 lb, has the necessary weight to absorb the recoil of a 1 oz load and therefore, in conjunction with a fair degree of choke, can be used to produce perfectly adequate patterns. In fact, at the pattern plate it would be impossible to say whether a full choke pattern with a 1 oz load came from a full-choke 12-bore or full-choke 20-bore. The differences would be so slight as to be negligible.

In the next chapter, it will be shown that minimum patterns or 120, 140 and 180 may be accepted for killing pheasants cleanly with shot sizes 5, 6 and 7 respectively. If we accept half choke as being the minimum necessary to control pattern quality, at a range of 40 yards with the 1 oz load a half-choke 20-bore will give patterns of 130, 160 and 200 and the full-choke 20-bore offers 150, 190 and 240. Both are more than adequate. The owner of a 20-bore over-and-under, fitted with multi-chokes to allow him to change from open to tight patterns, has nothing to fear in terms of gun performance and killing power.

4 PATTERN, SHOT AND CARTRIDGE

I have deliberately avoided using the word 'ballistics' in the title of this chapter. Like anaesthetics, ballistics put most people to sleep very quickly. However, when we claim the right to shoot live quarry we have to accept certain responsibilities and these include doing everything in our power to ensure clean kills.

To have a deep knowledge of ballistics the sportsman has to become something of a mathematician, engineer and scientist. This puts many people off the subject. It has been left to the sporting academics. Unfortunately, they don't always get things right and a large number of theoretical statements are found lacking when tried in the practical shooting field. Many of the finest craftsmen involved in the building of best guns have never fired a single shot. That is one thing, but it is an entirely different matter when the writings of certain self-styled ballistics experts leave the impression that they may never have held a gun.

Thankfully, in regard to ballistics, the practical sportsman need only concern himself with two major points. These are the striking energy of individual pellets and the overall pattern of the shot charge when fired. It is a combination of these two things, patterns and striking energy, which is decisive in killing cleanly.

Pattern is effected by the manner in which the muzzle ends of the internal walls of the barrels are finished. This is known as choke. The striking energy of an individual pellet is a result of its weight and its velocity. Many a shooting lunch has been passed in non-stop heated discussion for and against certain patterns, shot sizes and velocities. Equally, many a man, when suffering a bad patch in his shooting performance, will wonder whether a change of cartridge is all he needs to set things right. He might even better his previous performance. So what are the things we need to know about elementary ballistics?

Nature of the Pattern

Certain points must be understood about shotgun patterns. By general agreement, the pattern is defined in terms of the number of pellets that strike within a 30-inch circle at a given range. It can be expressed either as the number of pellets or, normally, as the percentage of the total charge. Therefore, if a gun is fired at a whitewashed steel plate and a 30-inch circle is drawn round the centre of where the charge strikes and it is discovered that, say, 150 pellets out of a total of 300 have hit inside the circle, the pattern would be describe as 50 per cent.

The pattern of shot spreads further and further as range increases and, therefore, if the gun is fired farther away from the plate the pattern will thin to, say, 40 per cent and, further again, to 30 per cent, and so on.

It is not just the number of pellets striking within the 30-inch circle which is important. Pattern quality must also be taken into account. The requirement is for an even spread of strikes over the area rather than a few clusters of shot with open spaces between them.

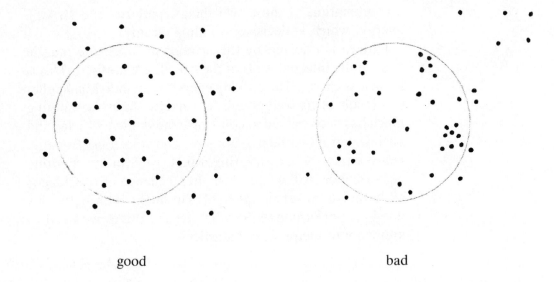

good   bad

*Pattern quality requires an even spread
of strikes over the area rather than a few
clusters of shot with open spaces between
them.*

The illustration shows examples of good and bad patterns.

It is also important to remember that, although we tend to think in terms of patterns as shown on a flat piece of paper, the pattern, in flying, has a three-dimensional form. We talk of the relative velocities of various cartridges, but some pellets will be flying a little bit faster than the bulk of the charge, and slower ones will be trailing behind it. The true shape of a shotgun pattern, when viewed from the side, is a teardrop.

This is something which we may have to make allowances for, because a bird flying across a theoretical circle may be struck by the leading pellets of the pattern but have

*Some pellets will be flying a little
bit faster than the bulk of the charge,
and slower ones will be trailing behind
it. The true shape of a shotgun pattern,
when viewed from the side, is a teardrop.*

passed on before the tail-enders have time to come up.
This stretching out of the pattern is known as 'stringing'
and, like the increased spread of shot, its effects are most
pronounced as range increases.

Choke

At one time, the internal walls of shotgun barrels were all
made parallel. Then it was discovered that by incorporating
'choke', a slight constriction at the muzzle of the gun, it
was possible to control and condense the shot charge so
that it did not spread so quickly.

41

The original parallel-walled barrel, which throws the widest spread, is known as true cylinder. A very slight constriction is known as improved cylinder and this goes through to the maximum beneficial constriction, known as full choke.

The idea behind all this is that the tighter the constriction, and therefore the smaller the spread of shot, the more strikes there are in a 30-inch circle. With choke, it becomes possible to throw as tight a pattern at 50 yards as the true cylinder throws at 30 yards. Therefore, the bird will be hit with just as many pellets, and the range of the weapon is significantly increased.

Whatever the degree of choke, the pattern continues to spread as the range increases, as is shown in the following table giving the diameter of shot spread from the six standard degrees of constriction at various ranges. Thus it is seen that with, say, a quarter choke, the spread increases by about 1 foot diameter for every 10 yards of range and that for long range work the full choke at 40 yards is able to throw as tight a pattern as the true cylinder at less than 30 yards. However, this also means that the tighter chokes require a higher degree of accuracy. A man may be a few inches off plumb centre and still hit with nearly 4 feet of spread from a true cylinder at 30 yards but, with

Diameter of Shot Spread

Range in yards	Diameter of spread in inches					
	True cylinder	Improved cylinder	Quarter choke	Half choke	Three-quarter choke	Full choke
10	20	15	13	12	10	9
20	32	26	23	21	18	16
30	44	38	35	32	29	27
40	58	51	48	45	42	40

little more than 1 foot of spread from a full choke at 20 yards, he must be spot on.

Choke and Pattern

It is very important, at this stage, to recognise that as far as a gunsmith is concerned choke is purely a mechanical matter. If asked to make a barrel with full choke, he will produce it with a constriction of forty thousandths of an inch. Ask him to measure the degree of choke in a barrel and he will use a barrel gauge to determine the exact internal diameter of the muzzle. A true cylinder will measure 0·729 inch throughout the barrel, because the walls are parallel. A half choke is constricted at the muzzle to 0·710 inch and a full choke to 0·693 inch.

The reason why this is so important is that *the degree of choke may bear little, if any, relation to the pattern thrown.* I have seen a gun that, although bored to full choke, threw a greater spread of shot than what one would expect of a true cylinder at 30 yards and, conversely, a quarter-choke gun that threw tighter patterns than would be expected from a three-quarter choke.

There are a number of reasons involved in this, tied up with the darker side of ballistics engineering, but all the practical shooting man needs to know is that he can easily be misled and it really doesn't matter what the barrel gauge says, it is the pattern plate that counts.

Testing and Regulating Pattern

The pattern thrown by a shotgun is tested at a range of 40 yards by firing the gun at a whitewashed steel plate. Rather than simply measuring the diameter of the total spread of shot, the test is conducted to ascertain what percentage of the total shot charge is thrown into a circle of 30 inches diameter. The wider the spread, the more open the pattern and the smaller the percentage.

The test is usually conducted with a $2\frac{1}{2}$-inch standard-velocity cartridge containing $1\frac{1}{16}$ oz of shot. Sometimes you will see tables of figures stating exact percentages for various patterns at different ranges. If you happen to believe that 1 per cent here or there will make the slightest difference to shooting performance, and if you believe that a gunsmith will indulge his time and effort and your money in shaving off the tiniest amount to bring a barrel to throw a 72 per ceent pattern rather than 73 or 74 per cent, then such tables may be of interest. However, a barrel seldom throws the same pattern twice and what we are talking about is averages. Therefore in the following table I have rounded the recognised figures up or down to the nearest 5 per cent. In my view, there are far too many people in the world, and particularly those involved in shotgun ballistics, who measure with the breadth of their hand or with a piece of string, and then give the results to five places of decimals!

In case anybody should think that a mistake has been made, the figure of 40 per cent for both quarter and half choke at 50 yards is correct, the exact figures being 38 per cent for quarter and 41 for half. This suggests not only why guns are tested at 40 yards rather than at longer range but also that, as range increases, so the effect of choke decreases – an important point to note. As can be seen

Shotgun Patterns

Range in yards	Percentage of shot charge					
	True cylinder	Improved cylinder	Quarter choke	Half choke	Three-quarter choke	Full choke
30	60	70	75	80	90	100
40	40	50	55	60	65	70
50	25	35	40	40	45	50

from the table, at 30 yards the difference between true cylinder and full choke is 40 per cent, which decreases to 30 per cent at 40 yards and to just 25 per cent at 50 yards.

Pattern for Pheasants

The ever-present risk in studying the ballistics of shotguns is that the application of theory may drive common sense out of the window. There is a danger of working to absolute minima when what we should be doing is allowing adequate allowances for error, human or mechanical.

In arriving at a suitable pattern for killing pheasants, it is necessary to follow a sensible course between having, on the one hand, not enough pellets to ensure a hit on a vital organ in the bird and, on the other hand, having so many pellets that the bird is cleanly killed but also plucked, drawn, minced and way beyond being ready for anybody's table. How do we determine the required pattern to ensure sufficient strikes? The method, if not the mathematics, is simple. We can calculate that the area of the 30-inch circle that we have been using to test the barrel's pattern is about 700 square inches. Equally, we can measure the area of a plucked pheasant, ignoring the wings, and discover that it is about 35 square inches; a cock is slightly larger and a hen a little bit smaller.

As the pheasant, flying overhead, fills one-twentieth of the 30-inch diameter circle, we can say that for every 20 pellets in the circle there will, on average, be one hit on the pheasant. If there are 40 pellets in the circle, there will be two hits, and so on.

So all we have to do is to decide how many pellets must strike the bird and from that decide how many pellets must be in the circle and, therefore, for a given total number of pellets in the shot charge, what percentage pattern we require to be thrown from our barrel. That may not seem too difficult, but the truth is that we are about to enter a veritable minefield of opinion and dogma.

A serious problem in deciding a proper pattern for the clean dispatch of pheasants is that over the years many writers have simply repeated the mistakes of others. However, because the ability to achieve clean kills is so vital to the sportsman, I personally feel that the subject is worthy of some hard consideration and discussion.

One of the most famous authorities on guns, cartridges and ballistics was Major Sir Gerald Burrard, and his words and thoughts have been accepted as gospel, forming the basis of many ideas on shooting in fairly recent times. He was human, however, and I believe that he made some significant mistakes in deciding minimum patterns required to kill game.

In Volume 3 of *The Modern Shotgun* he makes the statement that a pattern of just 60 pellets in a 30-inch circle is sufficient to kill a cock pheasant. What makes this all the more astounding is that he adds: 'If anything the patterns given are on the high side: but in working to a minimum it is ever better to play for safety rather than to suffer disappointment.'

Well, I am afraid that anybody accepting this advice will certainly suffer disappointment. What he is suggesting is that the smallest shotgun, the tiny ·410, firing less than ½ oz of shot from an open-bored true-cylinder barrel, will kill a pheasant cleanly at 40 yards – the overhead height of the highest-flying birds which can only be shown on a handful of well favoured shoots. And this is patently nonsense. To kill so high a pheasant with ½ oz of No. 6 would be nothing more than the very chanciest of flukes.

Where did Burrard go wrong? Well, it certainly seems strange that Burrard deliberately ignored the earlier findings of Dr Hammond-Smith. This is particularly strange because Burrard acknowledged the doctor as having greater experience than any other man in post-mortem examinations of shot game and said that his opinion deserved the greatest respect, backed as it was by his professional medical training.

Hammond-Smith's findings suggested a *minimum* pattern of 5 pellets of shot striking the bird, requiring at least 100 pellets of shot in the 30-inch circle.

However much Burrard may have known about guns and cartridges, this knowledge does not seem to have extended to a familiarity with the internal anatomy of game. The vital organs – the head, neck, heart, lungs and major blood vessels – occupy a very small part of the body. Three pellets striking the entire body are hardly sufficient to ensure that one of those organs will be hit, as Burrard said, but the five pellets of Hammond-Smith would be normally capable of ensuring a kill.

Other evidence was available as to the number of hits required on a pheasant in order to kill it cleanly. Again, this was based on post-mortem examination. Sir Ralph Payne-Gallwey in his book *High Pheasants* described 'twenty exceptionally high pheasants and how they were killed', his conclusion being that though four or five pellets may strike a very high pheasant it is a mere chance if one of them enters a vital part with sufficient force to kill and that to have a good chance of killing a high pheasant at least seven or eight pellets should strike it since, on average, not more than two of this number are likely to hit it in vital places. These findings were published in 1913.

It is impossible to know why Burrard, twenty years later, chose to ignore both Hammond-Smith and Payne-Gallwey, but he did. It seems very strange that a man who should work to such exactitudes in the matter of gun and cartridge should appear to fall back on guesswork and hunch when it came to what many would consider as the most important aspect of all – the ability of gun and cartridge to kill cleanly.

My own feeling is that Burrard, in this particular respect, can be ignored. Hammond-Smith, with his pattern of 100 pellets in a 30-inch circle, was, as he stated, suggesting a minimum. Payne-Gallwey, whose 7 or 8 hits require a pattern of 140 to 160 pellets in the circle, went beyond that to suggest a pattern which, so long as it was centred on the target, would practically ensure a clean kill.

Some may suggest that adopting Payne-Gallwey's figures is like taking a sledgehammer to crack a nut. However, it is important to realise that it is only averages that are being discussed, and that a pattern of, say, 100 will sometimes produce five hits, sometimes six, and sometimes as few as four or even three. It is at these low figures that game may be wounded rather than killed cleanly.

If you have ever patterned a gun on the range, firing at a whitewashed steel plate, you will know that in practice, as opposed to theory, patterns are seldom evenly spread. Many patterns will show areas where the shot is concentrated and areas where it is spread very thinly.

The two diagrams should make it clear that in practice a bird flying in the upper right quadrant may be hit by as many as six or even seven pellets, and therefore hit stone-dead, but a bird in the lower half of the circle may be hit by only one or two, and fly on wounded. This is unnecessary. We should at least *try* to kill our birds cleanly.

Pattern quality is dependent upon a large number of factors and varies from gun to gun and cartridge to cartridge and with various shot sizes. With a combination of gun and cartridge that throws as near perfect theoretical patterns as possible, we might be prepared to go for a pattern that throws 120 pellets in the circle, but with the standard weapon – the one which, after all, we all use – an extra 20 or 40 pellets will go a long way to ensure that what we hit is killed cleanly.

I think it is very important to acknowledge that inadequate patterns do not miss birds; what they do is wound them. How can anybody shoot confidently when they cannot be sure, even when a pheasant is

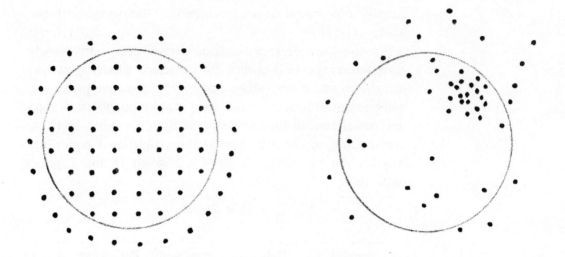

theoretical   practical

In practice, a bird flying in the upper
right quadrant may be hit by as many as
six or even seven pellets, and therefore hit
stone-dead, but a bird in the lower half of
the circle may be hit by only one or two,
and fly on wounded.

plumb centre in the pattern, whether or not it will fall?

Pellet Size and Striking Energy

So far, pattern has been discussed only in relation to the degree of spread. However, besides boring a gun to throw tighter patterns, there is another way to increase the number of pellets in the circle. In fact, there are two. You can use a smaller size of shot and, therefore, have more pellets for a given total load or, equally obviously, you can increase the weight of the load.

For the sake of brevity, shot sizes 6 and 7 are widely accepted as the best choice for pheasant shooting and so just these, and a size either side for comparative purposes, will be considered. Also for comparative purposes, Italian and American shot sizes are included in the table, as these are the major cartridge-producing countries besides the English. In the text, all sizes are given in the English equivalent.

Shot Sizes

English	Italian	American	Pellets per oz
5	5	6	220
—	6	—	240
6	—	—	270
—	—	7	300
7	7	7½	340
8	8	8	450

It might appear from the table that No. 8 would be the size of shot to choose, but because each pellet of shot must have sufficient striking energy to penetrate this matter has to be looked at in greater depth.

Striking Energy

The striking energy of a pellet is in direct relation to the weight of the pellet, which remains constant, and its velocity, which decreases with range. The following figures are for a cartridge with a standard mean velocity of 1,070 feet per second.

The decision that now has to be made is what figure can be accepted as the minimum striking energy in order to

Striking Energy of Individual Pellets in Foot-pounds

English size	Range (yards)				
	30	35	40	45	50
5	2·6	2·2	1·9	1·6	1·4
6	2·0	1·7	1·4	1·2	1·0
7	1·5	1·3	1·0	0·9	0·7
8	1·0	0·8	0·7	0·5	0·4

ensure adequate penetration. Burrard made suggestions as to minimum striking energy that related only to small, medium and large game birds. These, respectively, were 0·5, 0·85 and 1·5 foot-pounds. Many people have interpreted his figures as saying that snipe need only 0·5, geese will require 1·5 and practically everything else, from partridges to black game, are lumped under the heading of 'medium', requiring 0·85 foot-pounds as a minimum. Does this make any sense?

Is it possible to compare a cock pheasant weighing in at 48 oz, or even a hen at about 35 oz, to a cock partridge at 14 oz or a grouse at 24 oz, or, come to that, a woodpigeon at 18 oz? The pheasant is not only twice the weight of the other birds but has a stouter breastbone to protect the vital organs in its chest. That is why, for pheasants, a cautious increase in minimum striking energy up to 1·0 foot-pound seems logical.

On the other hand, where we are achieving patterns in the order of 180 pellets in the 30 inch circle, the chances of hitting the head or neck are increased, and so it may be possible to get away with a minimum of 0·85 foot-pounds. From this table I hope it is clear that No. 8 shot can be discounted. What it gains in numbers it totally loses in striking energy. Its use would lead to pheasants being

Maximum Effective Range in Yards

English size	Minimum striking energy (foot-pounds)	
	0·85	1·00
5	65	60
6	55	50
7	45	40
8	35	30

struck with very large numbers of pellets – a night-mare for the dinner table – but beyond a relatively short range the pellets would be unable to penetrate sufficiently.

Comparative Patterns

For the sake of brevity, certain adjustments and allowances have been made in the tables of comparative patterns which follow. No. 8 shot has already been discarded on the grounds of insufficient striking energy. For the same reason, no figures have been given for ranges over and above that at which shot sizes fail in regard to striking energy – for example, 45 yards for No. 7 shot. In this instance, for those who rely on hitting the head or neck, the figure taken as a minimum is 0·85 foot-pounds.

Only patterns from a minimum of 80 to a maximum of 220 have been included. This covers the entire range from slightly less than Dr Hammond-Smith's suggested minimum to rather more than Sir Ralph Payne-Gallwey's maximum, at which clean kills are almost guaranteed. To exceed this figure of 220 creates the problem of 'overkill', as discussed later.

Shotgun Patterns: Pellets in 30-inch Circle with $1oz$ or $1\frac{1}{16}oz$ Load

	SHOT SIZE		
	5	6	7
	Pellets in charge		
	230	290	360
Range in yards	Pellets in 30-inch circle True cylinder		
30	140	170	220
35	120	140	180
40	90	120	140
45	—	90	120
	Improved cylinder		
30	170	210	—
35	140	170	220
40	120	140	180
45	100	120	150
50	80	100	—
	Quarter choke		
30	180	220	—
35	150	190	—
40	130	160	200
45	110	130	170
50	90	110	—
55	—	90	—

Half choke

30	190	—	—
35	170	200	—
40	140	170	220
45	120	140	180
50	100	120	—
55	80	100	—

Three-quarter choke

30	210	—	—
35	180	220	—
40	150	190	—
45	130	160	200
50	110	130	—
55	90	100	—

Full choke

30	—	—	—
35	200	—	—
40	160	200	250
45	140	170	210
50	120	140	—
55	90	120	—

It may seem surprising that the tables purport to cover both the 1 oz and 1 $\frac{1}{16}$ oz loads, far and away the most popular choices for game shooting. You would expect, certainly in theory, that the heavier load would produce a slightly denser pattern. However, the few extra pellets are, in practice, cancelled out by the fact that the 1 oz load, fired from a 12-bore, produces the finest patterns in terms of distribution. In practice, therefore, the differences are so tiny as to be unworthy of attention. At the end of the day, some people have great faith in the 1 oz load – it certainly minimises recoil and is first choice for lightweight guns – but others have their confidence improved by a few extra pellets.

Finally, because we are dealing with averages rather than exactitudes, the figures normally given in tables of this sort have been rounded up or down to the nearest ten.

An Acceptable Balance

Mention has already been made of two schools of thought on the minimum striking energy required. If the subject is approached purely in terms of penetration through the breastbone and into the chest cavity, it seems that a minimum of 1.0 foot-pounds may be required. However, it is also possible to concentrate on the head and neck, when a minimum of 0.85 foot-pound is all that is required.

Naturally, if a sportsman subscribes to the 'head and neck' school of thought, he requires to have a denser pattern in order to increase his chances. Those who go for the chest need something with more punch, but, because the target area is rather larger, they no longer need such a close pattern.

It might seem sensible to accept a standard of, say, 140 pellets – rather more for when the striking energy is at a minimum and slightly less when the shot's penetration is not in question. And, by a happy coincidence, we see the figures 120, 140 and 180 repeating themselves through the tables of shotgun patterns.

This suggests that, irrespective of shot size, a true cylinder pattern with 1 $\frac{1}{16}$ oz of shot has a maximum effective range of 35 yards, which, let it be said, covers the needs of most pheasant shoots in this country.

If the patterns are tightened slightly to improved cylinder, the effective range, still irrespective of shot size, is pushed out to 40 yards. Quarter choke makes very little difference to this figure, half choke being needed to squeeze the range out to 45 yards.

When we go beyond a range of 45 yards, No. 7 shot lacks the striking energy even for the 'head and neck' school of thought, but with either No. 5 or No. 6 shot and a full-choke barrel it is possible to gain another 5 yards of range and reach the magical 50 yards.

The Medium-High Pheasant

Nobody should shoot at a short-range pheasant, so the question and answer seem to lie between a gun capable of taking medium-high pheasants and one which will kill the very tallest and most testing of all. Why not simply use the same gun for both? If a choice of pattern and shot will kill at 50 yards, why not use it for all pheasants, irrespective of range?

First, the table of the diameter of shot spread (page 42) shows us that at a range of 20 yards – and 60 feet overhead is a good pheasant on most shoots – the shot spread of a full choke is only 16 inches whereas that of a true cylinder is 32 inches. Therefore at such a range it is twice as difficult to hit a pheasant with a full choke. Also, if the pheasant were hit at that range with a full choke, what would be the effect? Catastrophic would be a good way to describe it. Even at 30 yards, using a full choke and No. 7 shot, the full charge of shot, all 361 pellets of it, would strike within the 30-inch circle. Therefore, the pheasant would be struck by, on average, 18 pellets. Remember, at the end of the day, somebody is going to eat that bird.

In fact, on the average shoot, any pattern of more than improved cylinder used with No. 7 shot will mean that any pheasant at less than 35 yards is likely to suffer severe overkill.

Truly High Birds

There are very few shoots that can regularly produce birds at heights in excess of 100 feet but, where they can, open patterns are incapable of killing cleanly and should not be used. Quarter choke seems so much of a 'betwixt and between' that it hardly merits attention, and so we are left with half, three-quarter and full choke.

One or two things must be understood about high pheasants. First, and most obviously, it takes an outstanding shot to hit them with any sort of regularity. Second, and probably most important, high pheasants have the habit, just like high duck and geese, of being either hit or missed by yards. A few inches here or there makes little if any difference. At a range of 40 yards, a half choke has a spread of 45 inches, only 5 inches more than a full choke. Personally, when shooting really high birds, I would happily sacrifice those few inches in order to gain the full choke's rather denser pattern, and for the same reason I would choose No. 7 shot. Logically it might be hard to justify No. 7, since by choosing No. 6 or No. 5 I could expect to gain another 5 yards in terms of range. But I have heard so many experts in the shooting of high pheasants singing the praises of No. 7, and have used this size so much, not only for pheasants but for duck as well, that I have the utmost faith in it. Just as in the choice of a gun, confidence in a shot size leads to concentration, competence, and successful shooting, and any pheasant over 40 yards, 120 feet high, outside the range of No. 7, is a very rare bird indeed.

High Velocities, Heavy Loads and Hard Shot

Besides the standard game cartridges containing 1 oz or 1 1/16 oz of shot, there are a number of alternatives on offer. First, there are the high-velocity and heavy loads.

Taking velocity as a starting-point, the idea behind these cartridges is that they will have a higher striking energy. The standard cartridge has a velocity of 1,070 feet per second, against the high velocity of about 1,120 feet per second. The effect, getting down to exact measurements, is that the striking energy of No. 6 shot at 45 yards is increased from 1·2 to 1·3 foot-pounds. There is also said to be a slight saving in the forward allowance required. Again at 45 yards, the standard-velocity needs 9 feet 6 inches, but the high-velocity is slightly less, 9 feet 1 inch to be precise.

What this gain of 0·1 foot-pounds and 5 inches has to be weighed against is that, particularly with barrels bored to throw open patterns, an increase in velocity is one of the factors that leads to poorly distributed patterns. Unless something of the order of half choke or more is used, tighter chokes helping to control pattern, the loss in pattern quality is likely to outweigh any other marginal advantages.

Then there are heavier loads, 1 ⅛ oz of No. 6 or 7 shot often being seen as potent medicine for high pheasants. Well, even in the case of a full choke at 45 yards, the difference in the number of pellets striking within the 30-inch circle is 8 more for No. 6 shot and 10 for No. 7, which means only that the pheasant, well covered by a 1 or 1 ¹⁄₁₆ oz load, will be occasionally hit by one more. However, once again, this is even less likely than it seems because just as an increase in velocity tends to upset patterns and their even distribution, so does an increase in the load.

There is one more factor in regard to faster, heavier loads which cannot be ignored. They increase recoil. The optimum ratio of gun weight to shot load is generally accepted as 96:1. In other words, if you have a 6 lb gun and fire a heavier cartridge than 1 oz shot load you will be aware of recoil. Similarly, it takes a 6 ¾ lb gun to comfortably handle the 1 ⅛ oz load. Even if you have a 6 ¾ lb gun, by using a lighter cartridge you effectively reduce the recoil to a practically negligible level and this can lead to important gains because, as the recoil is hardly noticeable after the first barrel is fired, the second barrel can be got off quicker and more effectively.

If it seems that there is no place for heavy, high-velocity loads in pheasant shooting, except when used in particularly heavy guns, probably over-and-unders, with tight chokes which help to control pellet distribution, there are at least two other possibilities that cannot be dismissed as lightly. These are hard shot and plastic monowads, where the shot is contained in an open-ended plastic sleeve.

The argument for hard shot and monowads is that one factor affecting the density and quality of patterns is that those pellets on the outside of the charge, those in contact with the barrel wall on their passage to the muzzle and through the choke, are subject to friction. They are distorted and do not fly true to the mark, nor as quickly as the bulk of the charge. This is how stringing of the charge in flight is increased. If harder shot, more resistant to distortion, is used, or if the shot is protected by a plastic sleeve, a greater number of the total pellets will fly true, and stringing can be reduced. Thus, in a cartridge which incorporates a monowad or hard shot, the pattern density may be increased by as much as 10 per cent. However, although such benefits may at first seem significant in terms of killing at extreme range, the truth is that at, say, 45 yards we are only increasing the number of pellets striking a pheasant by one, on average, when it is already struck (theoretically) by 10 pellets of No. 7 shot.

The arguments against hard shot are mainly concerned with its extensive use in guns of a certain antiquity because it could hasten the final wearing out of the barrel walls. However, with newer guns, considering the thousands upon thousands of rounds of hard shot fired by some competitive clay-pigeon Shots in a season without any apparent ill effects to their gun's barrels, this argument is put into its proper context. The arguments for and against plastic sleeves concern fairly marginal ballistic performance at one level, but for sportsmen in the field they seem to centre round the litter problem.

At the end of the day most sportsmen will be happy to stick with standard wads and shot except perhaps for those few occasions when the prospect of really high and testing pheasants convinces them of a need to squeeze the last few grains of performance from their weapons. Even then, rather than the performance of their guns, it is really their own confidence that they are boosting.

5 GUN FIT AND OTHER MATTERS

This chapter could very well have been entitled 'Suiting the Gun to the Individual'. Indeed, in many ways, choosing a gun is very similar to ordering a suit from a tailor. In Chapter 3, the conclusion was eventually reached that, in all probability, the best choice of gun will be a double-barrelled hammerless 12-bore in the side-by-side style. In fact, relating that to the ordering of a suit, all we have done is choose the weight and pattern of cloth. We also had a look at barrel length and gun weight – the equivalent of deciding whether the suit should be double-breasted or single-breasted.

The general outline is now firmly established, and all that remains is to fill in the details. In the case of a tailor, he will ask what width of lapels is required, how many and which pockets, wide trouser bottoms or tapered, with or without turn-ups, with or without waistcoat, and so on, right down to whether a button or zip fly is required.

Similarly, decisions will have to be made on trigger configuration and whether the stock is to be a straight-hand or pistol grip. Should it be an ejector or non-ejector, and would there be real advantages in a self-opener? Is the style of rib important to the individual? And so on.

In the case of a suit that is bought off the peg or a mass-produced or second-hand gun, it will largely be a case of looking for the style or model which most closely fits the customer's desires and requirements. This can lead to a need for compromise.

Finally, and probably the most important of all, in the case of either a suit or a gun, is that it must either be made to measure or, if it is not being made expressly for the customer, be as close a fit as possible so that it can be made as near perfect as possible with the minimum of alterations.

Triggers

Traditionally, the vast majority of side-by-side game guns have been made with double triggers. The great advantage, it is said, is that this allows the shooter to choose which barrel he will fire, where he has had one barrel bored to throw tighter patterns. Therefore, if he is shooting a bird that is departing, he will first pull the front trigger to fire the right, more open barrel, and save the tighter pattern of the left barrel, fired by the rear trigger, in case he needs a second shot at greater range. If the bird is approaching, as in the case of driven game, he should use the rear trigger first.

Of course, for the driven shooter, this does mean adopting a rather unnatural habit, because it is always easier to fire the front trigger first, but the wise shooter will practise at the shooting school until he gets this right.

The alternative is a single trigger but, unless it is selective, this means that the shooter is stuck with firing the two barrels in a set sequence. Also, single triggers do not have the same reputation for reliability as the double trigger. One could say that there are tens of thousands of over-and-under guns being used for clay busting, and these seldom give any trouble. All I can say personally is that I have experienced malfunctions with single triggers, and have thanked God that it didn't occur on the best stand of the finest day's shooting. Game shooting puts severe demands on a gun. It is in the tight corner, when barrels get so hot that a glove must be worn on the left hand, that guns will inexplicably malfunction, rather than in the relatively calm conditions of shooting clays that are presented as and when called for.

And so, for a game gun, I personally would go for double triggers every time.

Choke and Pattern

The relation between choke and pattern has been explained in the previous chapter. If a gun is to be used solely on driven pheasants, and on the general run of pheasant shoots, where a really high bird is one passing 25 yards overhead, nothing more than true or improved cylinder is required. Many men will seek a little of both, and have true patterns from the right barrel and improved in the left. On better than average shoots, rather stronger medicine is required, with a combination of, say, quarter and half choke squeezing the effective range out that little bit further.

To allow for both types of shoot, and to have a gun that is equally effective for rough shooting, a compromise is reached. A gun with improved cylinder in the right barrel and half choke in the left has long been advised for the 'take anywhere' standard game gun, the jack of all trades.

Finally, there are those shoots, just a handful, that can consistently produce absolute scorchers of birds. They justify the adoption of three-quarter and full chokes.

Personally, with the multi-choke gun having become so popular with over-and-under users, I am amazed that at the time of writing none of the more common models of Spanish side-by-side guns are offered with this option. The multi-choke is, in effect, a tube which is screwed into the muzzle of the barrels. Different tubes throw different patterns. Thus, effectively, the owner of a single gun can, in a minute or so, change from, say, true and improved cylinder to three-quarter and full choke.

The design of multi-chokes has come on apace to the stage where, unless you actually look into the muzzle, it is very hard to detect their existence, so the essential lines and appearance of the gun are not effected. If the fact that the barrels are side by side rather than over and under causes any minor engineering problems, they are surely surmountable, and *if* there were any minor effects on gun balance, surely this would be outweighed by the advantages of one game gun to cope with anything?

There are great advantages to be gained in doing as much of one's shooting as possible with just one gun. The user becomes totally familiar with its feel, handling and balance.

I read somewhere, quite recently, an article by a top clay shooter which stated the advantages of, and how to use, multi-chokes for shooting a round of sporting clays. It surprised me that he concluded that they would only have very minor advantages for a game gun. I cannot agree. Certainly, if one were to shoot nothing but driven pheasants of average height, they might hold little advantage, but when, like me, you mix this shooting with other close-range work such as woodcock in cover, duck coming into a flight pond, bolting rabbits with spaniels, and so on, and then go on to really high pheasants, roosting pigeons, and flighting duck and even geese, let alone that second shot at fast-departing late-season grouse, you can see a hundred and one advantages for a gun with multi-chokes. If nothing else, at the very least, we would no longer have to shoot rear trigger first when shooting approaching driven game with double triggers.

I cannot believe that it will be very much longer before multi-chokes are available on side-by-side guns. When they are, I for one will be taking a very close look at them.

Straight-Hand or Pistol Grip?

When using double triggers, the hand slips back slightly to bring the index finger back onto the rear trigger. It is far easier to slide back on a straight-hand stock, so the straight-hand is always best for this trigger configuration.

On single triggers, the hand does not need to slip back and a pistol grip can be incorporated to give a marginally steadier grip. The general rule, therefore, is that a straight-hand should always be a feature of a gun with double triggers but is optional on a single-triggered gun. Some find that even if the pistol has the better grip they prefer to do without it as it spoils the flowing lines of the gun. Again we see the appearance of the gun, and how it effects the user's confidence, being placed at the top of the list of desirable qualities.

Under the same heading, it is possible to consider the fore-end of the gun. Besides a few heavy weapons, designed for wildfowling, it is rare to see a beavertail fore-end on a side-by-side, except in America. To European eyes, these broad and clumsy additions completely ruin the appearance of a gun. Their purpose, it is said, is to protect the left hand from the barrels when they are either too cold or too hot to handle. European shooters would prefer to use a glove, or a leather handguard on the barrels.

Ejector or Non-Ejector?

When the top lever of a gun is pushed over, the barrels drop and, in the case of a non-ejector, the cartridges have to be picked out with the fingers. This is a fiddly task at best and far worse with numb fingers in cold weather. A gun fitted with ejectors throws out the fired cases, thus giving a great saving of time in reloading.

In fact, nowadays, apart from a few guns of fairly advanced years, it would be rare to find any gun that was not an ejector, except cheaper boxlocks intended for the rough shoot, farm and foreshore.

Self-Openers and Easy Openers

In the standard ejector gun, the barrels must be pushed down with the left hand after the top lever has been pushed across. In a self-opener, when the lever is pushed across, the barrels drop by themselves. Thus, with a self-opener only the right hand is required to unload the gun and the left hand is free to snatch two more cartridges from the cartridge belt or pocket. A man practised in the use of his self-opener can put up a tremendous rate of fire, approaching that of a man using two guns and a loader – if he keeps it up for a sustained period, firing from just one gun, he will soon be able to fry eggs on the barrels.

The few critics of self-opening guns base their arguments on the fact that, as every schoolboy knows, to every action there is an equal and opposite reaction. The mechanism is operated by a spring which is compressed in closing the gun. This makes for what somebody described as an 'easy opener, stiff closer'. However, this small degree of stiffness in closing the gun is easy to get used to, and those who use self-openers to their full potential swear by them. Besides a number of best English guns, some imported models, including the AYA No. 2 sidelock, are now offered with this option.

It should be noted that an easy opener is not the same thing as a self-opener. In fact, guns described as easy openers are a sort of halfway house between the self-opener and the standard gun. They are easier to open than the standard, but the barrels still require at least a nudge from the hand and, therefore, it has to be asked whether any benefits that they are said to confer are at best marginal, if not doubtful.

Rib and Foresight

Few shooting men take an interest in the rib and the small bead foresight on their guns, certainly not for game shooting. They probably assume that it does not matter at all how they are formed, because a shotgun should be pointed rather than aimed, or, if they do matter, the gunmaker will know best.

However, these things *are* important because it is visual as well as mechanical pointability which really scores. On the other hand, if the degree of visual pointability is just that little bit too much, it can encourage the shooter to aim rather than swing. A compromise has to be reached and, thankfully, we find that the gunmaker does actually know best by incorporating a high, narrow, file-cut rib of the Churchill type on guns with short barrels; a plain, hollowed rib on standard barrels; and just occasionally, for those who like to take their really high birds, be they pheasants, duck or whatever, with a high degree of precision almost tantamount to aiming, high, broad, flat-topped and file-cut ribs on long barrels, with maybe a slightly larger bead for the foresight.

These comments on ribs apply only to side-by-side guns. When you are about to fire and looking down the barrels of a side-by-side, the grooves at either side of the rib show as dark lines and the blued barrels disappear. However, because the sides of the rib on an over-and-under are not thrown into shadow, the rib will nearly always be of the broad, flat, file-cut type.

Trigger Pulls

Before looking at the fitting of a gun to the individual, there is just one other matter that needs to be mentioned.

It has been left to this stage because it is not a fixture to the gun but an adjustment. It is the weight of the trigger pulls.

If the trigger pull is too heavy, it will take something approaching a conscious effort to fire the gun. This will normally lead to a miss behind as the hesitation causes the gun to falter in its swing. On the the other hand, it may lead to a miss in front if the time lapse between the brain saying 'fire' and the cartridge being detonated is extended.

At the other end of the scale, very light trigger pulls, equivalent to hair triggers, are decidedly dangerous.

The happy medium is normally found with a trigger pull that is half the weight of the gun. Thus, on a 6½ lb gun the trigger pull should be set at just over 3 lb. That is for the front trigger. When the finger moves back to the rear trigger there is generally more leverage and thus the rear trigger should be about 25 per cent heavier than the front, at about 3¾ lb.

Whatever the weight of gun, if the weight of the trigger pulls are kept in these proportions, the pull will *feel* exactly the same. With some wildfowlers who specialise in geese the mighty 8-bore is still popular. A 12 lb double would be considered almost as a lightweight in this class of weapon. Its front trigger would be set at a pull of 6 lb, but it would actually *feel* no different from a 5½ lb 20-bore trigger pull set at 2¾ lb. Strange, but true.

A man who suspects that his trigger pulls have gone astray can easily test them with the type of scales used for weighing a fish. A snap cap is placed in the chamber of a gun, because it is ill advised to drop the hammer on an empty chamber. The hook on the scale is hooked around the trigger, and a gentle pull applied until the gun goes 'click', a close eye being kept on the needle on the scales to note the exact weight of pull required.

As long as the pulls are approximately right the man using a single gun should not worry too much, but if, as I once found on an imported off-the-peg gun weighing 6¾ lb, the front trigger pull is set at 2¾ lb and the rear trigger at over 7 lb, a visit to the gunsmith for adjustment is obviously required.

For the man using a single gun, then, the trigger pulls need not be exact, so long as they are in the right proportion. For example, the suggested trigger pulls of 3¼ and 3¾ lb on a 6½ lb gun could just as easily be 3½ and 4 lb respectively without causing any undue upset in performance. With a pair of guns, however, the situation is very different and where the pulls are even marginally different between the two guns their owner, firing one after another, will be well aware of the fact. He will feel that one weapon has clean, crisp pulls but the other feels long and dragging. That is why the sidelock, on which the pulls can be adjusted very accurately, became the first choice of a man requiring a pair of guns for driven shooting. The most finely adjustable of all trigger pulls are on the best English guns.

Fitting the Gun

It has been said that the fit of a gun is as important as the fit of a suit. In the same way that it is impossible to feel comfortable in ill-fitting clothes, trying to squeeze a 44-inch chest into a 40-inch jacket, so nobody can shoot his best if he is, say, a tall man with a short-stocked weapon. However, the big difference is that, whatever a country gun dealer may say, it is impossible to fit a gun to an individual simply by measuring his vital statistics or watching him put up a gun at some point on the ceiling of a shop. What is happening then is that the gun is being aimed in the manner of a rifle, rather than pointed. Fitting without actual shooting can only be an approximation, and therefore it must be done at a

The try gun is used to measure the individual's requirements with regard to stock length, bend and cast.

shooting school with the measurements being taken off a 'try gun'. Even a tailor requires his first and second fittings.

The Try Gun and Essential Measurements

The most essential measurements of a stock are its length, bend and cast. On a try gun, which any shooting ground worthy of the name should have, the stock is adjustable to each of these measurements, as can be seen from the illustration.

The shooting coach, being experienced in these matters, will be able to judge the individual fairly accurately, and set the stock of the gun to at least a rough approximation, a starting-point, from which minor adjustments can be made.

Even if it is a blazing hot afternoon in July, the shooter being fitted must wear the clothes in which he will be shooting in November. A gun that fits when the shooter is wearing a shirt and light pullover will be found to be rather long in the stock when a heavy jumper and jacket are worn to keep out the cold.

Normally, the coach will take the shooter to a place where he can shoot at a whitewashed steel plate with a life-size outline of a bird fixed to it. The shooter will be told to fire at this bird, quite naturally and without dwelling on his aim. After a series of snap shots have been fired in this way, the coach will have a fair idea of any initial adjustments that need to be made. However, where the skill of the coach doing the fitting comes into play is that for each and every possible error there may be a number of causes and solutions.

For example, if the pattern of shot has consistently been striking below the target, there may be too much bend in the stock, but it could be that the trigger pulls are just a bit too heavy or the shooter's left hand is not far enough forward to support the barrels. If, on the other hand, the pattern is striking high on the target, there may not be sufficient bend, the stock may be too long or have more 'toe' than necessary, or it could be that, for the individual, the trigger pull is set too light.

With a right-handed shooter, if the pattern is striking on the right it may be that there is too much cast-off and if it is on the left there may be insufficient; but it might also be that the stock is respectively too short or too long, or that the shooter is simply not bedding the gun accurately into his shoulder. There must be a high degree of consistency in gun mounting before a man can be properly measured for a gun, and the coach may feel that some instruction in this regard is necessary before the fitting is taken any further.

Incidentally, for the technically minded, gun fitting is not inspired guesswork on the part of the coach. Depending on the distance from the eye to the muzzle – and let us assume that this is 36-inches, which is exactly 1 yard – when the gun is then fired at a range of 20 yards from the plate any faults at the gun end will be multiplied by twenty times on the plate. For example, if the pattern is being thrown with a centre 12 inches above the point of aim, the stock is probably far too straight and, if so, the bend can be increased by a twentieth of 12 inches, which is 0·6 inch.

By now the coach is getting a very fair idea, but he will be well aware that there is a temptation to aim rather than point at the plate, and so he will move the shooter to a stand to shoot some fairly straightforward clays.

Straightforward going-away or low approaching shots can tell a certain amount about the bend and cast of a gun's stock, but faults in the length can be obscured by the shooter compensating by moving his left hand up or down the barrels slightly. What will show up faults is to take an overhead shot. The coach will look for any check in the swing, which may indicate that the stock is rather too long, as it will if the stock is obviously catching on the jacket as it comes up to the shoulder. As a check, the coach may ask the shooter to take the next shot with the rear trigger. If he finds this more comfortable, and the swing is no longer checked, then the stock obviously requires to be a little shorter.

And so it goes on. The coach may have the shooter trying some shots at long crossers. A good coach can actually see the shot in the air and, if it is consistently flying too high or low, he will know that more adjustments are required. Eventually he will declare that he has arrived at his final judgement. He will then be able to report back to the gunmaker or, if he is independent, to give the measurements, taken off the try gun, to his shooting client.

Options

The shooter, having a list of the measurements for a stock which will best suit him, now has a number of options open to him. At the top end of the market, the chosen few who can walk into the premises of a London gunmaker and order a new gun will probably have been at the gunmaker's own shooting ground, or one closely connected. A gunmaker likes to *know* that the measurements have been taken properly before he sets about investing considerable thousands into a new gun for his customer.

Leaving these aside, a man may decide that he does not wish to pay the high price for a 'best' English gun but nevertheless wants a gun made to his exact specifications. Some Spanish firms, such as AYA, will make guns to an individual's measurements and specification in such matters as barrel length and, within reason, final gun weight, and so on.

Alternatively, the man may decide that he will purchase a second-hand gun and look for one which is as close as possible to his own measurements. Of course, it does not need to be exact. Stocks can be shortened by sawing or shaving, and can be lengthened with a block of timber, carefully matched to be as close as possible to the timber of the existing stock. Methods of clamping are used to increase or take away cast. But, obviously, major alterations should be avoided whenever possible. For example, a 6-foot 4-inch right-handed man will be fairly wary of a gun built for a left-handed jockey, and so on.

The Next Stage

Once a gun has been made to specification or been adapted, it should be taken to the shooting grounds for a final check. Normally the fit will be as good as expected but other matters need to be looked at. For example, are the patterns thrown by the gun equivalent to the nominal choke boring? For another, are both barrels shooting true to the point of aim? Believe me, this is not always the case. The right barrel may be spot on, but the left barrel can be firing low and off to the side. In either case – faulty patterns in terms of distribution or point of aim – a cure can be effected by a barrel regulator. In truth, if I were ordering a foreign gun to my own specification, even if I wanted improved cylinder in both barrels, I would ask for full chokes and have the gun regulated here upon delivery.

It may be that the gun is found to be perfect in all respects, or it may be that it will have to go back to the gunsmith for some adjustments. In either case, the final stage of gun fitting must be a good long session of clay busting, which will ensure the happy owner's complete confidence in his weapon so that he can use it to its, and his, full potential in the field.

Changes in Fit

It has been said that the shooter should always wear his normal shooting clothes when being fitted for a gun. For some, in terms of pheasant shooting, this may involve a heavy pullover, a thick quilted waistcoat and a tweed topcoat. That constitutes a fair amount of bulk, and therefore the stock is made that little bit shorter.

The problem may then arise that the shooter decides that he can afford, or is lucky enough to be invited, to start his season early with a visit to the grouse moor in August or the partridge manor in September. He is hardly going to wish to don the cocoon of heavy clothing that he deems necessary for the gale-torn December pheasant shoot. But, with a shirt and light jacket, his stock will be too short and his shots may be pulled off to the right, or low, or both.

Thankfully, a short stock can be compensated for by moving the left hand slightly farther up the barrels. It is a trick regularly used by those who review guns for magazines and the like. Goodness knows, when I was editor of a sporting magazine and a steady stream of guns came through my hands for inspection, my left hand was tromboning constantly. That is sufficient to meet with most eventualities on the majority of moors, where the birds hug the contours on relatively level ground, but other moors are full of gulleys and ravines that can produce magnificent sport with high grouse. Equally, particularly where partridges are driven over belts of pine trees rather than hedges, overhead shots will again be taken, and it is the overhead shot and the high crosser which really expose faults in stock length. A very simple solution is to use one of those slip-on recoil pads to bring the stock up to the desired length. In this case it is far easier to add than to take away.

Another problem, which is not so easily solved, is variations in the physique of the shooter. By that I do not mean that the gun is being lent to a friend but, let's face it, as we go through life there is a tendency for our chests to fall to what we once proudly called a waist, our shoulders to sag and . . . well, that's probably enough to be going on with. Some men enter their later years as fit as a fiddle, but others are a shadow of the strapping figure they cut in their late twenties or early thirties, the age at which they had their guns fitted. A falling off in performance may be due to nothing more than a change in physique. If this is suspected, a trip to the shooting grounds for a session with the try gun and coach will confirm or deny whether this is really so.

How Important Is Fit?

When I gave up reviewing guns in order to get down to some serious shooting, I truly believed that the 'average'

75

gun, taken off the peg, was the right fit for myself. In fact, all that had happened was that I had learned to adapt myself to the gun, rather than actually having the gun suit me. I kept on thinking that way until, having a chat in a gunsmith friend's workshop, I was having a look at a gun that had been fitted to a fairly tall man. When I say tall, I mean that I am a whisker over 6 feet and he has 4 inches on me. So, as can be imagined, the gun had a good long stock and, because the man had a long neck, a high degree of bend.

Now, I thought I had rather a short neck. It seemed short to start with and, after a wee accident on the Rugby pitch after which it was rebuilt by neurosurgeons, it seemed shorter still. However, as my gunmaker friend pointed out, getting my hair cut a bit more regularly would soon remove that impression.

Anyway, I mounted the gun and was amazed to find that while the stock was obviously a bit too long and the bend a little too high the gun felt very comfortable. In fact I was no longer having to adopt an almost straight left arm and the stock came up to my cheek rather than my having to tilt my head down to it.

We discussed this at some length and decided that we should go through the standard try gun procedures without any preconceived notions, and with myself trying to shoot in as natural a style as possible. I would have to try hard to avoid what might have become an ingrained habit of fitting myself to a gun, any gun.

The outcome was that we discovered that the gun which by then had become my firm favourite for all forms of game shooting, a Gunmark Viscount, a gun that had 'standard' stock measurements, was not only about ¾ inch too short in the stock but also required a good deal more bend and a whisker more cast, reflecting the fact that I am rather taller and with a longer reach than the average, and fairly broad in the shoulder. The only thing to set me apart from a gorilla was the slightly longer neck!

The alterations were made in about a fortnight, and I quickly discovered that my shooting was greatly improved. The most marked difference was where the gun had to be shot almost instinctively – say, on woodcock flitting through cover, duck dive-bombing into a pond in the last trace of light, or pheasants whistling across a forestry ride – but it even made a difference on medium-high pheasants which, one might have thought, gave plenty of opportunity to adjust to an imperfectly fitting gun. Experiences such as this underline advice and confirm that there is no substitute for a gun stock fitted to the individual's needs and physique.

6 CLOTHES, EQUIPMENT AND GUN CARE

The majority of modern country sportsmen look as if they have just fallen off a production line. Come rain, hail or shine, at the game fair or county show, on a baking day on the August grouse moor or at the side of a windswept January pheasant covert, you will see them in their uniform. There are regiments, nay, brigades of flat caps, Tattersall check shirts, waxed jackets, moleskin breeches and green wellies on parade. And, very often, the result is what can only be described as lashings of sweat when honey-bees drone over the rolling purple oceans of heather and chattering teeth when the leaves have long fallen. Somewhere, of course, and some time, they must actually feel comfortable. But less of my sarcasm. Let's look at the alternative options.

The Shooting Suit

Traditionally, on the smartest shoots, a tweed suit of matching jacket, waistcoat and breeches is practically obligatory. I have such a suit. The man at Redmayne's in Wigtown, Cumbria, who supervised the 'building' of it from design and specification to final fitting was quite

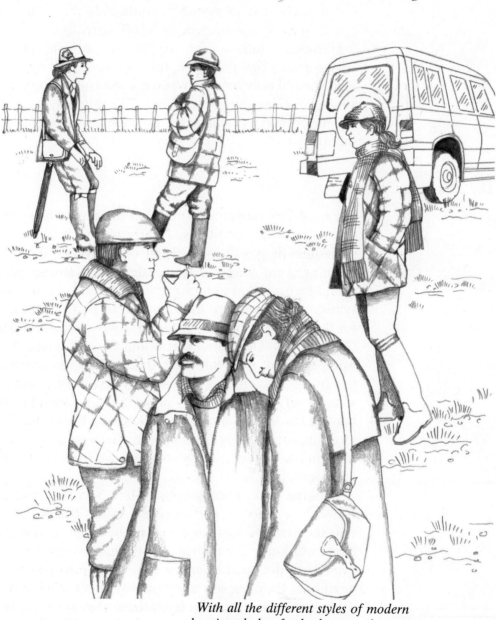

With all the different styles of modern shooting clothes for both sexes, the accent is very strongly on warm, wind- and waterproof.

insistent that as much as it should be functional, it should also be 'elegant'. I have a sneaking suspicion that this was a diplomatic way of saying it would hide the bulges. The price? Well, it was the suit or 5,000 cartridges.

However, much as I regard this suit as ideal for early-season grouse and partridge, for pheasant shooting it tends to fit the bill only on days when it is pleasant to be out and about, on calm days of sunshine. The simple fact is that it lets in too many draughts for the general run of pheasant shooting.

The Shooting Coat

Pheasant-shooting conditions seem to fall into two general sets of weather conditions. Nearly always it is cold, and sometimes it is wet as well. In olden days, when those shooting were likely to be gentlemen of leisure, shoots would be cancelled in prolonged heavy rain. Today, when syndicate shooters are hard pushed to find ten Saturdays for their sport, a cancelled shoot is a loss that often cannot be made up. They simply grin and bear it, whatever the weather conditions throw at them. And so, nowadays, the accent in clothes is very strongly on warm, wind- and waterproof. However, it is important to remember that, bar the occasional shower, it is keeping warm that is the most important thing. This is particularly important to the man on the driven shoot, who may have to stand about for long periods.

Looking back, photographs of late Victorian and early Edwardian shooting parties reveal things besides the fact that they tended to wear eccentric headgear and mutton-chop whiskers. Back then, long before antibiotics had even been dreamed of and a chill could lead you to your deathbed, they knew a thing or two about staying warm. Today we talk of jackets. Back then, they spoke of tweed coats that covered the nether regions and fastened high at the neck. This had the added benefit that lapels were kept

Standard clothing for the shooting man.

to a minimum and well out of the way of the gun stock when mounting to fire. Also, the coats were fitted with roomy patch pockets to hold a good supply of cartridges and other odds and ends.

Today, the waxproof jacket is very similar in design. It has the advantage of being waterproof. However, it is not warm nor is it pleasant to the touch. This cannot be said of tweed. A tweed coat, of the Husky Tweed Coat style, is far better for the average shooting day. Tweed is warm and windproof, very pleasant to wear, and will hold out all but prolonged rain.

The best course therefore, if funds will allow, is to have a tweed coat as the main protection, with a waxproof in reserve for those times when the shoot is held in really heavy rain.

Because all that water has to go somewhere off a waxproof coat, and that somewhere is straight onto the wearer's thighs, leggings or, better still, overtrousers should be worn with this jacket in rain. The type with zips running up the calves of the legs are very convenient for slipping on and off.

Quilted jackets are popular as outer garments and serve well on calm, crisp days. However, because they are neither totally windproof nor remotely waterproof their use is limited.

Under the Coat

If a man is after the full tweed-suit effect he will have a waistcoat made in the same material as his coat and breeches. However, the modern sportsman and his tailor seem to have forgotten the principal purpose of a waistcoat. They treat it rather like the handkerchief used for 'show' rather than 'blow'. Otherwise why would the back be made of such flimsy material? Next time I am passing the tailor's, I will ask whether it would be possible to have a tweed-fronted waistcoat run up with a quilted back, having plenty of overlap at the waist band.

This leads on to the enormously popular quilted waist-coat of the Husky type. Under the coat, they are warm, light and comfortable. Because they have no sleeves, they avoid bulkiness at the shoulder and do not interfere with gun mounting and swing.

Under the waistcoat, wear as many layers of *thin* woollen pullover as necessary. Two thin layers of wool are far more warming than one thick layer.

Beneath that, the shirt should be of some warm and natural fibre, and it's up to the individual to decide on underwear. Many who use them swear by thermal vests and long johns for really cold days.

Breeches

Call them what you will, I shall call them breeches. The choice is really between moleskin and tweed. For the driven shoot, tweed is that little bit smarter, and smartest of all when the material matches that of the tweed coat. Incidentally, if going to a tailor, have him make two pairs of breeches, as they wear out in half the time of the coat.

If buying off the peg, the style of the breeches will be pre-ordained. However, from a tailor you will be asked whether you want what they describe as plus-twos or plus-fours.

For those of an inquiring mind, when hanging unfast-ened, what the tailor calls breeches will reach just below the knee, plus-twos will reach mid-calf and plus-fours almost to the ankle. The plus-four is really a baggy piece of kit, with a circumference of more than 2 feet at the knee, and the plus-two is by far the better choice.

Hat, Scarf and Gloves

'If you want to get ahead, get a hat' goes the old saying, and, because birds will swerve at the sight of a bare fore-head or bald head, this saying is particularly true for the shooting field.

83

Gone are the days when men shot wearing top hats, homburgs or bowlers. Today, first choice is a flat tweed cap. If it rains, a towelling scarf keeps water from running down the back of the neck. In heavy rain, have two towelling scarves so that they can be swopped at lunch.

Any hat with a brim at the back may have a tendency to catch on the jacket collar, particularly when shooting high overhead birds, which are difficult enough even when your hat *isn't* tipped over your eyes. However, some like their deerstalkers, although those with earflaps and a steeply dropping back brim can be a nuisance. Some like the old felt hat that their grandfather wore to race meetings, while others take things to extremes and do impressions of Stewart Granger in the film *King Solomon's Mines*. At least these white-hunter affairs keep their wearers dry, acting like an umbrella.

A towelling scarf, as said, stops water running down the neck and either one of these or a woollen scarf is a boon on a cold day.

Gloves are a real bone of contention. It seems that the need to be as thin as possible so as not to interfere with the feel of the gun and trigger, and for picking up cartridges, is wellnigh incompatible with adequate warmth. Personally, on really cold days, I have come down to wearing a pair of the thinnest kid leather gloves, on which the trigger finger can be turned back, and a heavier lined pair of gloves over these. I remove the outer gloves at a drive just as soon as I expect game to appear. If the ideal shooting glove has been designed, I have yet to see it.

Socks and Boots

Shooting socks are interesting. In a world where shooting men are beginning to all look the same, the shooting sock seems to be the last expression of individuality. Most will be greens and browns but, particularly with younger Guns, there will be a spattering of blues and reds, canary yellows

84

and salmon pinks. It's all good fun and, with wellie boots, only the tops are seen. The best thing to keep them up with is woven gaiters, as worn by the Highland regiments, rather than any sort of elastic affair. Failing that, an old pyjama cord, cut in two, will serve quite well if tied in a bow rather than a granny-knot.

If rubber boots are being worn, the life expectancy of the heel of a woollen sock is about one day. Slip on a light pair of nylon socks over the wool.

Having mentioned rubber boots, it has to be said that in a perfect world we would all wear leather boots or stout shoes. However, they are not much good for fording streams and wallowing through gateways churned into a sea of mud by cattle and tractors.

Boots of the fairly lightweight 'green wellie' type are very good so long as they are a reasonably comfortable fit, neither too tight nor too slack. They should really be tried on when wearing both the wool and nylon socks, and with an insole inserted. A fairly thick insole, in addition to that supplied in the boot, will go a long way towards keeping the feet warm.

As for those rather twee belts and buckles on the sides of the boot, I cannot see any useful purpose for them. They catch in anything that is available. The last pair I bought even had small metal crowns sticking out of the sides. One morning, on the banks of a stream, having caught my fishing line and landing net a dozen times or more, the crowns were ripped off and belts and buckles fell foul of a sharp blade.

Gun Case and Sleeve

A case is ideal for protecting the gun when it is being carried to and from the shoot. On arrival at the shoot, the gun is taken out of its case, assembled, and immediately placed in a gun sleeve, or slip, as it is sometimes called.

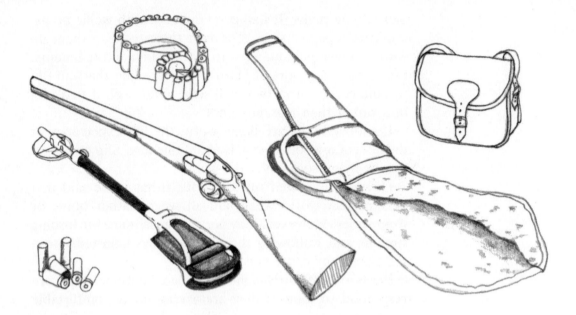

Basic equipment for the pheasant shooter:
cartridges, shooting stick, gun, cartridge
belt, sleeve and bag.

Sleeves are either canvas or leather, real or imitation. They are either unlined or lined with a fleecy material. Those with a fleecy lining must have a zip running for their full length so that if they get wet they can be opened out to dry. Their advantage is that the lining gives slightly more protection if, say, the barrels are knocked in the vehicles. Personally, I use a fleece-lined leather sleeve.

The criticism of the lined sleeve is that gun barrels, if wet, are more prone to surface rust. I really cannot see why this should be so but, even if it is, the sleeve is only for transporting the gun between drives, and the gun really shouldn't be left in *any* sleeve if it is wet. At the end of the day, give a wet gun a rub-down with a dry cloth, put it in its case, and take it out for a clean just as soon as you get home.

Cartridge Bag or Belt

Only a few men will be seen wearing a cartridge belt on a driven shoot. Think about it. It is not at all uncommon to find, taken over a day, that only one pheasant has been killed for every three or four shots fired, particularly if the birds are high and testing. Therefore if 100 birds are shot probably 300 cartridges have been fired, which means about 40 by each individual gun. Some will shoot more and some less. And it is rightly considered as something of a crime to run out of cartridges in the course of a shoot. Therefore, on a 100-bird day most men will consider 50 cartridges as the minimum to start off with, and they will probably have a reserve in the car for topping up at lunch time.

As a belt will only carry 25 cartridges, there is no alternative to a cartridge bag for driven shooting on anything but a modest scale. A big one is better than a small one and need not always be filled to the top. Leather cartridge bags, though more expensive than canvas, can be seen as a once-in-a-lifetime investment if properly cared for.

At the start of a drive, with two cartridges in the gun, a dozen more can be slipped in the coat pocket and, with the bag open on the ground, reserves are always to hand.

Incidentally, this is probably the place to mention my infuriation at manufacturers of waxproof coats who incorporate a sort of tube on the jacket pockets. This may make them even more waterproof, but renders them useless for fast reloading. It is a simple matter to cut them out and stitch them down.

Shooting Stick

A shooting stick with a broad leather seat is a necessity for those who find it uncomfortable or impossible to stand for

*A shooting stick with a broad leather
seat is a necessity for those who find it
uncomfortable to stand for practically an
entire day in the field. The safe gun position
is pointing in the air.*

practically an entire day in the field. And, for anybody, it is easier to sit, relax and stay fresh while waiting for the driven birds to appear. Against this, a shooting stick is a nuisance to carry if you are asked to act as a walking gun. On the other hand, there is seldom any lack of volunteers to borrow the stick and take the weight of their feet for a while. At the end of the day, whether to use a shooting stick, except for the elderly or disabled, is a matter of preference rather than necessity.

Gun Care and Cleaning

The order of precedence, on returning home, after hailing the family, should be dog, gun, and then self.

After drying and feeding your dog, check over and clean your gun. You will obviously need a cleaning kit. Those offered in presentation boxes have not changed since the days of our grandfathers. There are new and better products that we can use.

The cleaning kit is as follows: cleaning rod with jag and phosphor bronze brush; 4 x 2 flannelette patches, newspaper and tissues; toothbrush and tin of petrol as used in cigarette lighters; aerosol can of combination gun oil; small bottle of artist-quality linseed oil; and fouling solvent such as Parker Hale 009.

First, before ever you leave the shoot, give the gun a rub over with a dry cloth and spray some gun oil or WD40 down each barrel.

Second, on getting home, take the gun to pieces and clean out the barrels by pushing through rolled-up balls of tissue with the cleaning rod. Rub tissue paper up the sides of the top rib to remove any moisture. If the gun is dry you can move straight to the third stage, but if it has been wet, having removed as much moisture as possible, put the fore-end, barrels and stock next to a radiator to dry. The stock should be placed action down to let moisture drain out. The barrels should be placed muzzle down.

Get out of your wet clothes, say hello to your spouse, pour both of you a large malt then place yourself, face up, in a deep tub of hot water. By the time you emerge, the gun should have had a chance to dry and you can move on to stage three.

Clean inside the barrels thoroughly with 4 x 2 flannelette patches on the jag and cleaning rod. Check to see whether there is any fouling up the barrels. Whether lead or plastic, it should come away to a scrub with the fouling solvent and phosphor bronze brush. Repeat the flannelette treatment until they come out clean.

Fourth, clean around the breech end of the barrels and the action of the gun with a combination of an old toothbrush and petrol, taking care not to go on to the stock and remembering not to smoke. The petrol will quickly evaporate.

Fifth, place a soft cloth a few inches from the muzzle end of the barrels before giving each a good squirt of the gun oil from the breech end. Some of the oil will have sprayed on to the cloth, and this is now used to wipe down the outside of the barrels and the action.

Last, presuming the timber of the stock has an oil finish, put a couple of drops of the linseed oil on one palm, rub your hands together, and then give the stock a brisk rub.

Incidentally, before using the gun again, the oil that was sprayed into the barrels must be removed. This is done the night before the next shoot, with a rolled-up tissue.

What, you may ask, was the newspaper for? Well, maybe your spouse, like mine, will appreciate a few sheets laid here and there before you start spraying gun oil around.

Storage

The gun should be stored in some dry place that is as warm as possible. For security reasons, this should really be a steel gun cabinet. A few sachets of silica gel, as used in camera cases, will help to prevent moisture. The steel cabinet should not be anywhere that is exposed to direct sunlight, otherwise, come the cold of night, condensation can form.

At the End of the Season

A gun represents a considerable investment and should, at the end of the season, be serviced by a reputable gunsmith. If next season you find you have a malfunctioning gun, you will wish you had met the small cost involved.

After the gun has been serviced, it shouldn't be simply put away and forgotten about. It should be inspected periodically. As you give the barrels a quick rub over with an oily cloth, if nothing else it will evoke the memory of days past and fill you with anticipation for the season to come.

7 HOW TO SHOOT

The traditional way to learn to shoot and handle a gun was, quite simply, to go out and use one. The majority of shooting men of former generations would have been presented with a gun in their early or middle teens and, in the company of an experienced relation or keeper, would have learned the craft of shooting on a mixture of rabbits, pigeons and the occasional game bird walked up in the fields and hedgerows.

The emphasis was very much on learning the rules of safety. One transgression and the culprit would be marched firmly home, the gun locked away, and there would be no more outings until the lesson had been given plenty of time to take root. The pupil, therefore, became conversant with the rules of safety, which is absolutely essential, and learned something of the ways of the birds and the beasts. Instruction in how to shoot, however – the art of hitting a moving object – was very limited.

This was the way that I learned to shoot. I was given my first gun in my early teens and my father used to go out with me on the farm that stretched away from our house and down to the estuary of the Nith river.

I remember that I missed a pigeon with my first shot, got a right-and-left at snipe with my second two shots, then emptied the entire contents of a box of cartridges punching holes in the air around ducks and pheasants, partridges and pigeons, rabbits and hares. Eventually, I started to hit about one time in four. By my mid-teens, my father, who was an absolute stickler for safety, declared that I could at last be trusted to shoot on my own.

Now, I can tell you that even if this is the best way to produce safe shots, it is very definitely not the best way to learn to shoot. I was twenty-one before I received my first lesson at a shooting school, and bad old habits had become so ingrained by that time that the instructor had a thankless task. In fact, by the end of the session, he had improved my shooting a great deal but, a fortnight later, when my new gun came back with some alterations to the stock fit, the old habits had regained firm control. It took a considerable effort both in time and money at the shooting school to replace the old 'chuck it up and chance it' methods with something approaching a good and relatively successful shooting style.

So you could say that I have learned to shoot the hard way. But it is not the way that I would suggest for anybody else. Safety is, and always will be, of primary importance. The basic rules should be learned before a gun is ever handled. However, because it is so vital in terms of future performance, I would argue most strongly that the first place that anybody should fire a gun is at a shooting school, under the supervision of a good coach.

I spend part of each year instructing guests in how to cast with a fly rod. It is quite common to meet up with a husband-and-wife team. Often, before they arrive, I get a letter from the husband telling me that he has been fishing for many years, and has caught a few salmon, but his wife, although keen to at least try the sport, has never touched a fly rod. The implication seems to be that his casting only needs a little brushing up, with some time devoted to the Spey and roll as well as overhead casts, but with his wife I shall have a much more trying job on my hands. Well, let me tell you, after a few days the wife may well be casting as well, if not better, than her husband. It is so much easier to work on virgin territory, as it were, rather than trying to eradicate faults that have become ingrained over a number of seasons. And the real problem is to establish new methods so firmly that, even in a momentary lapse of concentration, they remain dominant. How many times have I seen a casting instructor working with a guest, getting his casting right, then, a few hours later, when the guest is actually fishing, the bad, old habits slowly re-establish themselves. It is exactly the same when teaching, and learning, to shoot.

Incidentally, in case you are wondering, I started to fish when I was a toddler, but with a float. When I started to show an interest in fishing the fly, my father's passion in sport, I was immediately taken to the Spey and instructed for a week by Captain Tommy Edwards and Jack Martin, both champion casters and great fishermen. At the age of seven I was never given the chance to pick up bad habits, certainly not with a fly rod!

The Basic Technique

There are many shooting techniques but, of them all, I believe the 'smoke trail' method is the best and easiest to start off with. It is very suitable for shooting driven pheasants and, once the basics of the technique have been mastered, it can be honed, perfected and adapted into a very effective shooting style. It is the one that I shall discuss in this chapter.

The most basic fact to be aware of in shotgun shooting is that, in order to hit a moving object, we have to point our gun's barrels in front of it. Certainly the charge of shot is moving very quickly at ranges up to 40 yards – the figure is a little bit more than 1,000 feet per second – but, even so, the bird will have moved on in the short lapse of time between the trigger being pulled and the shot arriving at

*The right hand is placed in a
comfortable position grasping the hand of the
stock from where the extended finger can rest
lightly on the trigger. This right hand should
be slightly under the stock in order to bear
the weight, and the thumb is curled round
to complete the grip with the fingers.*

the target. With a bird crossing in front or passing directly overhead at approximately 40 m.p.h. at 40 yards range, the bird will have flown 8 feet in that time.

Now, having given you some figures, I must immediately ask you to forget them. We need to be aware of the theory of forward allowance, but that is all. At no time should we be putting up our gun and thinking 'I shall aim 9 feet in front of the target'. The smoke trail method, as we shall see, incorporates these allowances automatically. But first, before we do anything else, let's pick up the gun.

The Hands

Whenever a gun is picked up, the top lever should be pushed over and the barrels dropped to check that it is unloaded. After that, we need to know how best to hold the gun in order to shoot with it.

Assuming that the man using the gun is right-handed, the trigger will be pressed with the pad, rather than the joint, of the right index finger. Therefore the right hand is placed in a comfortable position grasping the hand of the stock from where the extended finger can rest lightly on the trigger. Incidentally, the only time when a gun's trigger should be touched is in the moment before the gun is fired.

This right hand should be slightly under the stock in order to bear the weight, and the thumb is curled round to complete the grip with the fingers. Again, just before the gun is fired, when it is actually on its way into the shoulder of the shooter, the thumb will slip the safety catch forward, then immediately go back to its gripping position. If the thumb is left against the safety catch when the gun is fired the recoil may bring the end of the top lever onto the tip of the thumb, which will, at very least, be painful.

To look now at the left hand, this is the one that controls the barrels. It must hold the barrels in such a way that the view down them, the sighting plane, is not obscured. The

*King George V developed a fashion
for shooting with a straight left arm but,
although many have tried it, few have found
it altogether successful, particularly when
shooting high overhead birds.*

grip is like a loosely set vice. The barrels rest on the open palm and are pinched between the thumb on one side and three or four fingers on the other. The reason I say 'three or four' is that many shooters, myself included, prefer to have the index finger pointing straight up along the lower rib which joins the barrels. A shotgun is *pointed*, never aimed like a rifle, and it is far easier to point accurately with one finger than a fist. The position of the hand should be comfortable, which most men find means just in front of the tip of the fore-end. King George V developed a fashion for shooting with a straight left arm but, although many have tried it, few have found it altogether successful,

97

*The left arm should be neither too
straight nor too bent, but just comfortable.*

particularly when shooting high overhead birds, when it has
a tendency to pull the barrels off to the right. Neither is a
cramped position good style. With the hand too far back,
actually on the fore-end of a side-by-side, there is little
control of the barrels. As in most things involved with
shooting, the middle course is the one to follow, with the
left arm being neither too straight nor too bent, but just
comfortable.

Feet

The feet are said to be the basis of good shooting. This is
certainly true of driven shooting, even if wildfowlers and
pigeon shots will argue that they can shoot when sitting,

kneeling or even lying down. The fact is that if conditions and quarry allowed they would do a whole lot better by standing up and getting their feet working.

However, just as there is no one gun that will fit all men perfectly, so there can be no perfect stance. What may be right for a short, stocky man may be all wrong for his tall and lean neighbour. The accent should, very largely, be on what the individual finds most comfortable. Let me describe what I find the best position for myself, at 6 feet and a bit and what the tailor, very charitably, would describe as 'portly'.

To describe the position of my feet I shall start with both feet together. Then the right foot is moved about 6 inches to the side and then shuffled back about 4 inches and pointed at roughly 45 degrees to the left, leading foot. This is the basic position from which I feel best prepared to swing back and overhead or to either side.

The Ready Position

If I handed somebody a tennis racket and told him that I was going to throw a ball over his head and I wanted him to hit it, I wouldn't think of him as being very sensible if he stood with his arms at his sides and the racket head trailing on the ground. He has just been told where the ball is going so, surely, he should stand ready to receive it, with the arm raised and the racket head up.

Shooting, like hitting a tennis ball, is made very much easier when the shooter gives himself as much time as possible. At many shoots, even as birds are flushing, many of the shooters will be standing with their guns pointing at the ground. This is certainly safe, but no safer than pointing the gun up at the sky where the birds will be flying.

Having got the feet into the position already described, with the left foot pointing in the direction at which the shooter expects to take his shot, the left hand will point

99

*The ready position: the left foot points
in the direction at which the shooter expects
to take his shot, the left hand points the
barrels slightly above the tops of the trees
if the birds are being driven from a wood.
The stock of the gun will be resting
comfortably, tucked along the right forearm
of the shooter and against his side.*

the barrels slightly above the tops of the trees, assuming the birds are being driven from a wood.

The stock of the gun will be resting comfortably, tucked along the right forearm of the shooter and against his side. If the gun were to go off by mistake, the shot would fly harmlessly over the trees, so it is perfectly safe – a lot safer than swinging the gun up from a position pointing at the ground.

The First Shot

To restate an earlier point, in order to deny bad habits the chance to start, the first shot should be fired at a shooting school under the close supervision of a competent coach. Let me assume that it will be fired at a clay-pigeon thrown from a tower to pass directly over the shooter's head and about 50 feet up – a nice easy target simulating the sort of driven pheasant that experienced Shots will seldom miss. And, having made that assumption, let me imagine that I shall be taking the shot.

Standing in the ready position, with my barrels pointing just above the tower, I shall tell the coach that I am ready and he will call for the clay to be thrown.

As the clay shoots out of the trap and beyond where my barrels are pointing, I quickly imagine that the clay has left a smoke trail behind it, point the index finger of my left hand – and thus the barrels – at this at the same moment as my thumb slips forward the safety catch, swing up the trail, overtaking the clay, and, as the barrels swing through where the beak would be if clays had such things, squeeze the trigger. Really, this sort of shot is not so much a pleasure to hit as it is an annoyance to miss.

Because the gun was fired when it was actually pointing at the bird, it appears that no forward allowance has been made and the shot will miss behind. Why, then, was the

The gun comes up to the shoulder as
the target approaches. The barrels swing
through the target, overtaking it as the
trigger is squeezed.

clay powdered? As the clay had been picked up on its smoke trail, it was obviously necessary to accelerate the speed of the swinging barrels so that the clay could be overtaken. The brain says 'fire' in the instant that the barrels swing through the clay, making the shooter feel that he is firing directly at it. In fact, such is the reaction time between the brain saying 'fire', the message travelling down to the fingertip, the finger squeezing the trigger, the hammer falling and the detonator exploding, that in the fraction of time that this takes the barrels, still accelerating, will have actually pulled out ahead of the bird. Thus forward allowance is created automatically by turning the apparent failing of human reaction time to our advantage.

Gun Mounting

Gun mounting is the make or break of successful shooting. Therefore it is well worth giving it close consideration.

Starting with a shooter standing some little distance back from a wood, with his barrels pointing just above the canopy, on most shoots and on the majority of drives there will be a few seconds between a pheasant actually appearing and its being shot. Having decided that the bird is coming to him, the shooter simply points his left index finger, extended along the lower rib of the barrels, straight at the bird. Some men say that they imagine they have a very long bayonet on the end of their guns, and 'stick' the bird with it. From the moment the index finger locks on, that pheasant is a dead bird, or should be.

It is important to emphasise this point that the left hand, and the left index finger in particular, are actively pointed at the pheasant before the gun is raised to the shoulder. The bayonet analogy gives the right impression of a positive thrust at the bird.

It would be possible to track the bird as it passes overhead without ever raising the stock. This pointing method is how some shooters are able, quite literally, to shoot from the hip. However, outside the circus ring, what is necessary is to gently slip the gun stock up to the shoulder, scraping lightly up the right-hand front of the jacket the few inches required. The shoulder moves forwards slightly, the swing is accelerated, and the trigger pulled, all in one flowing motion.

Smoke Trail or Churchill Swing?

Robert Churchill was the gunmaker who popularised short-barrelled lightweight guns. Comparisons were made between these and the feel of a longer-barrelled heavier gun – rather like the difference between pointing a walking stick or a long fishing rod at an object. The stick is quicker to come up to the mark, but the rod is steadier when it gets there.

Let a man pick up a lightweight short-barrelled gun and mount it by pointing his finger at an approaching medium-high pheasant and he will find that the barrels are pretty well dead on target. It only takes the merest hint of a chuck ahead in the instant that the trigger is pulled to make the necessary small amount of forward allowance and the bird is hit. Now let the same man go through *exactly* the same sequence of gun mounting with a heavier gun, one with barrels of 29 or 30 inches rather than 25 or 26, and due to the inertia of the heavier gun he will find that he is a little way behind it, coming up its smoke trail. He must then accelerate through the bird and pull the trigger as he passes its beak.

To me, the only difference between the Churchill style of shooting and the smoke trail method lies entirely with the gun chosen. That is why I am against the practice that some men adopt of swopping from one gun to another. If they are most acquainted with short barrels and the Churchill style of shooting, they will probably miss behind when using a heavier, longer gun. If, on the other hand, they are more familiar with long barrels, they can easily miss in front if they turn to shorter barrels.

I don't know who started the rumour that it is impossible to miss in front, but it is absolute rubbish. I remember when a gunmaker sent me a beautiful little gun to try and I couldn't hit a thing with it. It was very close to my own gun's measurements in everything but barrel length and overall weight. And so I went off to a shooting school to discover where I, or it, was going wrong. After I had hit maybe two or three out of ten easy clays passing directly overhead, the instructor told me that these had been caught just on the trailing edge of the pattern and the others had been missed right out in front. After realising that, I started squeezing off my shots just as soon as the stock of the gun bedded into my shoulder, and I was hitting quite nicely after that. Problem was that, on the real thing, in the heat of the moment, I was back to my old ways and missing in front again. So I put the little gun away and got back to some proper shooting.

The point of all this is that, particularly on high, testing birds, the longer barrels have the more effective swing. Think of it like a golf swing. That tiny extra fraction of swing as the barrels are catching up with the bird is a great help to straight shooting, and it is easier to apply the desired forward allowance, on a really high bird, with a smooth accelerating swing than by arriving on the bird and having to simply 'chuck' ahead of it. In purely practical terms, it is no coincidence that the majority of top performers on high driven pheasants choose a minimum of 28-inch barrels, with many opting for 29 or 30 inches. The driven pheasant with its relatively stately progress is a very different target from the covey or driven grouse or partridge, which can come and go like lightning. While the shorter-barrelled weapon may be ideal on moor or manor,

With the overhead bird, it is not
possible to swing back to full extent without
raising one or other of the heels.

this does not mean that it will be anything like ideal at the covert-side.

Footwork

Smart footwork is an integral part of good gun mounting and, therefore, in the same vein, it is worth closer consideration. The good Shot should be up on his toes like a dancer or boxer.

Starting with the overhead bird, it is not possible to swing back to full extent without raising one or other of the heels. Some right-handed men will throw their weight onto the right, rearmost foot, and raise the heel of their left foot. Others will raise the heel of their right foot, and certainly to most eyes this looks the most graceful style. It is the one that I personally always shot with until I found that I had a distinct tendency to miss birds that came high but to my right rather than directly overhead. In fact, of course, I have a tendency to miss *all* birds, but these, I found, I was having particular problems with!

Again I went to the shooting school, and explained my problem to the coach. We decided that I should take a few shots and see what was going wrong. After I had taken a few clays from a position where the targets passed high and on my right, and had missed the bulk of them, the coach asked if I had ever tried raising my left heel and throwing my weight back onto the right foot.

Well, I tried it and it worked. What had been happening was that by raising the right heel to birds on the right-hand side I was effectively 'locking' my hips and body and, thus, swinging to my right was having the action of tightening a spring. And so, today, if a bird is coming to my left, or overhead, I throw my weight onto my left leg and raise my right heel, but if it is coming on the right it is the left heel that gets raised.

Naturally, all men are different but, if you are suffering problems with birds on either side, whichever heel you raise it may be worth considering adopting a variation in stance, as and when required. If you are a left heel raiser, and find problems with lef-hand birds, you might find that raising your right heel to those particular birds may work the trick, and vice versa.

The Going-Away Shot

Having gained a certain level of competence on the approaching overhead shot, most of us will wish to try some going-away shots at the shooting school. This time, the shooter stands close up to the clay pigeon trap which is

The rough shooter thrives on the going-away shot. It is the equivalent of a bird flushed by his questing spaniels, and it will also be encountered by walking Guns on the driven shoot.

109

set on the ground to throw clays away from the shooter's position.

This is the shot on which the rough shooter thrives, the equivalent of a bird flushed by his questing spaniels, and it will also be encountered by walking Guns on the driven shoot.

Pheasants, when flushed, will rise quite rapidly. They may not have the sky-rocketing flight of teal springing off a pond, but neither are they hanging about. If the gun is aimed directly at them, without allowing for the fact that they are rising all the time, they will be missed underneath.

The shooter should again imagine that they have a smoke trail, like looking after a low-flying jet rising slightly to hop a hill. The trail is not very extended in vertical terms, but it is there all the same. The gun is thrust at the bird with the index finger of the left hand pointing forwards to ruffle its tail feathers, accelerated up the trail and, as the body or clay is blotted out, the trigger is pulled. Again, the necessary allowance is automatic.

The Crossing Shot

Besides the approaching overhead bird and the one going away, there is one other bird to be encountered on the pheasant shoot. These are crossers, including those which curl across and in front of the line of Guns, those that fly outside the flank Guns and those breaking out at the side of a wood in front of a walking Gun keeping in line with the beaters.

In theory this should be the most straightforward of shots. From the ready position, it should be a simple exercise to imagine the bird flying with a smoke trail behind it, point the finger at the bird, mount onto its trail and accelerate through it, pulling the trigger as the swing passes through and beyond the bird's beak.

The problem is that there is a distinct tendency to 'rainbow' the barrels. For right-handed shots, this is usually most noticeable with a bird flying from left to right. Rainbowing occurs as a result of a dropping of the left hand. Swinging from left to right is against the natural flow of a right-handed shot. It is as if he were closing rather than opening the swing, tightening rather than uncoiling the natural flow, and down comes that left hand, taking the barrels with it, and the bird is missed beneath.

The only solution seems to be to make a very real conscious effort to keep the left hand up, taking a firm grip and steadying the swing with a distinct upward effort through the line of the bird. A useful exercise can be done in the privacy of the home. You stand facing a wall and imagine a pheasant flying along the line of where the wall meets the ceiling. If you are right-handed and imagine the bird flying from left to right, mount your gun on it and swing in a free and easy way; you will probably find your barrels rainbowing down off the line. Next time, make a conscious effort to keep the left hand up and see what a difference it makes.

Maintained Lead

Somebody, somewhere, may criticise me for introducing the idea of maintained lead, but I know that it has helped me when taking long crossing shots. We all find problems with one or two shots in particular and if, by adopting some other method, we are able to overcome them, then why not do it? Of course, if you never experience any problems with long crossers – maybe a shot at a bird that your neighbour has clipped but which is flying on – you need not read this section.

How I came to adopt this method on long crossers was, quite simply, that my conscious thought and intention was superseded by my subconscious. Put another way, I came to realise, when I analysed what I was really doing when I hit long crossers, that it was very different from the smoke trail method that I *thought* I was using. I think the first

111

time that I noticed it was when woodcock shooting when we lived in Cornwall.

Rather than accelerating through the bird, I edge ahead of it then swing for a few brief moments until I am sure the gun is just the right distance ahead – the target picture just right – before I pull the trigger. It should be noted that the barrels are kept swinging all the time to maintain the lead and, once that lead is established, there is no point in delaying the shot although, in theory, it could be held until the bird has passed out of range.

The problem is being able to recognise just how much the lead should be. Different people express it in different ways. Some say that they hold a gate's length in front of the beak. My own method, for what it is worth, is to think of it in terms of lengths of a cock pheasant. It has been calculated that at 30 yards an average crossing pheasant requires 5 feet of lead, and 8 feet at 40 yards. Therefore, if I judge the range to be 30 yards, I give a cock pheasant a lead of twice its body length, and if it is 40 yards I give it three times.

The great thing is to concentrate on keeping the barrels swinging at the right lead even after the gun has been fired.

It is necessary to make some adjustment if the bird is flying into or with a breeze – a little bit less or more. In fact, after a while, you stop thinking in terms of body length and develop a feel for the right sight picture. This is just as well. I would hate to think in terms of body lengths when faced with a crossing snipe at 40 yards!

Maintained allowance will be criticised by many shooting instructors and game Shots. If I did well on crossers at long range without it, then I would forget about it. However, those who choose to criticise it openly should remember that there was a time when the majority of Shots used this method, as described by Charles Lancaster. In a letter which appeared in *The Field* in 1886, an observer clearly noted that Earl de Grey (Marquess of Ripon), one of the greatest Shots of his and thus any era, shot in this way: 'when the pheasants afforded time, his lordship deliberately aligned his gun by swinging with the bird, often to the extent of several yards of its flight' and 'At the same time another excellent Shot (the Hon. Gore Booth) appeared to align, swing and shoot in the same style as above described.' Ah! There is nothing like a reference to a letter in the *The Field* of 1886 to kill an argument stone dead in the shooting field!

Having said that, whenever possible it is as well to steer clear of maintained lead, and it shouldn't even be contemplated if smoke-trailing or its shorter derivative is 'doing the business'. But it is a handy ace to carry up the sleeve.

8 SAFETY ON THE SHOOT

Unlike etiquette and behaviour on the shoot, which may not always be so obvious, safety is little more than common sense. And it starts with the realisation that as well as being a deadly short-range weapon that can rip through flesh and bone, maim and kill, a shotgun can also blind a person with a single pellet at 200 yards.

Accidents do happen in the shooting field. It is possibly something to do with the British character that we treat them so lightly, either brushing them under the carpet or treating them as a joke. I have been shot, and it felt like being hit with a baseball bat. Therefore I know that the beater who was struck in the ear at fairly close range would not have been amused when he was informed by the shoot organiser that they did not charge for ear piercing. Neither was a friend of mine, shooting in his home county of Norfolk, impressed with the comment of 'You'd better get that seen to' from the Gun who had just peppered him in the face. Three pellets were within half an inch of my friend's right eye. A very lucky escape.

I could go on listing shooting accidents. One of my relations was still a very junior doctor when a man was brought into casualty, half his face blown away, but still clinging to the fading, tortured embers of life. I know a man who had his arm blown off by an 'unloaded' gun as it was passed out of the back of a Land-Rover.

The reason I have described all these things is to underline that shooting safety must always be at the forefront of our conscious thoughts, and so deeply ingrained as to become part of our subconscious. You see, there is not one of the shooting accidents that I have described which could not have been avoided, and for which there was any excuse.

The following notes on safety relate directly to the shooting of driven pheasants.

The Unloaded Gun

On the driven shoot, the question of whether or not an unloaded gun should be carried open at the breech or closed should not normally arise. Guns should be taken out of their sleeves and loaded only when the shooters are standing in position for the drive to commence. As soon as the drive has finished, normally signalled by a whistle, the gun should immediately be unloaded and put back in its sleeve. Anybody who fires a shot after the final whistle has sounded should be heavily and publicly censured by the host and, if I had anything to do with it, would be sent home if he did it twice.

Awareness

After you arrive at the stand there will usually be a fairly lengthy time before the first pheasant appears. This time should be spent in checking where neighbouring Guns are positioned and, from this, working out safe angles of fire.

On the pheasant shoot, because the birds are well up in the air, safety angles are rather different from those on, say, a grouse moor. On low birds, if a line was drawn through three neighbouring Guns, the middle Gun would have two 90-degree sectors directly in front and behind where he could consider it safe to fire, and a

*These are safe positions to carry an
unloaded gun. Guns should be taken out
of their sleeves and loaded only when the
shooters are standing in position for the
drive to commence.*

*A dangerous shot. Not only are low
birds unsporting to shoot at, but they can
also be dangerous where Guns are standing
in line.*

90-degree sector on either side in which it would be unsafe.

However, on the pheasant shoot it may be possible to shoot a bird travelling in the 90-degree side sectors, just so long as it is well up in the sky. For this reason, because it adds the third dimension of height, some shooters like to imagine a solid four-sided pyramid between themselves and their neighbours.

That has dealt with neighbouring Guns, but they are not the only ones at risk.

Pheasants, when approached by a line of beaters, often prefer to run rather than fly. When they reach the end of the wood, if there is a handy hedge, they will hot-foot down this. In order to block this escape route, a 'stop', one of the more experienced beaters, may be sent to stand close up to the wood, but close in to the hedge. Equally, he may have been there since the crack of dawn to discourage birds from going out into the fields to feed. Whatever, have a close look about to see where stops, if there are any, are lurking. Pickers-up with their dogs are something else to watch out for. Sometimes they have to stand fairly close up to the line. At other times the odd individual can be very stupid.

I remember shooting at a field trial for retrievers where on one drive I and a neighbouring Gun were asked to take our partridges behind and drop them into a fairly small patch of rough cover. Birds were literally skimming between us, we turned to fire, and both shouted at the same instant. I couldn't believe it. Over my muzzles I saw, in what had been empty space for the last twenty minutes, an elderly lady with her labrador. Our shouts of warning to each other not to fire were as nothing compared to what the judge and stewards said when they discovered that, having arrived late, she walked up the back of the hedge and decided to stand just 40 yards behind the Guns, because 'her eyesight was not what it was and she wanted to see what was going on'. And, would you believe it, it

A dangerously low shot in front. Safe shooting requires allowing for all eventualities and never, under any circumstances, firing a shot where you can't be sure of the background.

turned out that she regularly picked up on shoots in her home area.

If there are horses, cattle or sheep remember that livestock do not know the rules of shooting safety and are likely to run about and pop up in the most unlikely places.

Take some time to consider where the beaters will be coming from. It may be that, where a wood is planted on sloping ground, with the beaters coming in high above the Guns, the birds must be left until they are overhead. Equally, ground game is likely to break from a wood only when the beaters are well up, just inside the

119

When loading a gun, the barrels should
be kept pointing at the ground and the stock
raised with the right hand to close the breech.

wood, and for this reason many hosts state at the start of the day that rabbits and hares are to be allowed free passage.

Basically, a sense of awareness is concerned with allowing for all eventualities, only taking those shots which are known to be totally safe and never, under any circumstances, firing a shot where you can't be sure of the background – be it the wood itself, a public road, a hedge or even a bush. Nobody on a pheasant shoot should be firing low shots anyway; all should be after the high bird with a background of clear sky. Remember that shot can ricochet off trees and branches, and not even a woodcock is worth anybody being blinded by a stray pellet. I was hit in the face only last season when what appeared to be a perfectly safe shot for a fellow Gun zipped off the treetops. Luckily, it did no damage, but it gave me quite a shock.

Always remember that, while we all harp on about loaded and unloaded guns, and how to carry them safely, the enormous majority of shooting accidents occur when somebody is simply tempted into taking a shot when he is not absolutely certain of its safety.

Loading the Gun

Most people one sees out shooting load the gun, dropping two fresh cartridges, and then close it by lifting the barrels. This is wrong and it is dangerous. The barrels should be kept pointing at the ground and the stock raised with the right hand to close the breech.

Carrying a Loaded Gun

> Never, never let your gun,
> Pointed be at anyone;
> That it may unloaded be,
> Matters not the least to me.

121

*The only safe place for a gun to be
pointing is at the ground or in the air.*

These are the first four lines of 'A Father's Advice To His Son' by Mark Beaufoy. And this rule should be strictly adhered to on the shoot, whenever the gun is taken out of its sleeve.

The only safe place for a gun to be pointing is at the ground or in the air.

Probably the best way to hold the gun when waiting for game to appear, when either standing or sitting on a shooting stick, is with the butt on the hip or thigh, barrels pointing up and forwards. This is perfectly safe and ready to come into the prepared stance for gun mounting and shooting.

When acting as a walking Gun, to shoot any birds that break out at the sides or which are going back, the shooter may carry his loaded gun in the crook of the arm, with

A walking Gun may carry his loaded gun in the crook of the arm with the barrels pointing at the ground. Alternatively, the right hand can grip the small of the stock with the barrels resting against the shoulder.

the barrels pointing at the ground. Alternatively, the right hand can grip the small of the stock with the barrels resting against the shoulder. Always keep the right hand tucked right in to the chest, otherwise the barrels will drop and anybody behind is in danger.

Incidentally, apart from the fact that he should never shoot at those birds which are going forwards to the line of Guns, the walking Gun has other responsibilities to observe. You will probably be told to keep in line with the beaters. If so, it is best to ask the beater closest to you to remain visible, right on the edge of the wood, and to ask him if he wouldn't mind carrying any birds you hit, leaving you free to shoot the next ones. Remember the possibility of ricochets off branches and only shoot your birds when they have a background of clear sky.

Responsibilities

Time was, we are told, when a shoot host would publicly admonish any offender against the codes of safety, etiquette or behaviour. If he offended twice, he would be sent home. Naturally, in the way of human affairs, this treatment was more likely in the case of a young relation than in that of a senior statesman!

Today, shoot organisers seem less prepared to accept responsibility for these matters. On commercial shoots, things can be taken to extremes. I am still wondering what went on behind the scenes on a certain grouse moor where a highly important businessman was being entertained. He shot two beaters before lunch. In the afternoon, with one diplomatic warning having been given, he went on to pepper his neighbouring Gun, the Gun's wife and another man, with one shot. This is not a story; it actually happened. He got a rather severe talking to, and was then allowed to shoot on the next day. Somebody could have been killed.

At the end of the day, such men continue to shoot in company only because the company allows it. Of course, it is embarrassing to make a fuss. That was the way I felt one day when I was a lot younger and glad to have been invited to a good shoot – so glad that I felt I could not say anything to my host about my neighbouring Gun. But from the moment he loaded his gun and put it over the crook of his arm with the muzzles pointed straight at me I knew he was a dangerous Shot. And, of course, he turned out to be jealous and greedy as well. My day ended on the fourth drive when a rabbit ran between us, on a narrow forestry ride, and I was carted off to have the shot pellets taken out of my leg and side.

Today, while still being fully aware of my responsibilities to my host and fellow Guns, I am also aware of my responsibilities to myself, my wife and my children. Therefore, if I find myself next to a dangerous neighbour – and most of them are so thick-skinned as to pay no heed to hints or even statements along the lines of returning their fire – I would have a quiet word with my host, explain the situation, say that I am prepared to develop a diplomatic illness if necessary, but that, if the situation continues, somebody is going home.

The last lines of Mark Beaufoy's advice read:

> All the pheasants ever bred,
> Won't repay for one man dead.

It is my own feeling that the sooner safe, responsible shooting folk take those words to include themselves as well as others, the sooner the day will arrive when the dangerous, greedy Shot is no longer tolerated.

9 SHOOTING ETIQUETTE AND BEHAVIOUR

The rules of shooting etiquette and behaviour are so closely intertwined with aspects of safety that it is tempting to treat them as one and the same thing. And yet, just as no elderly lady will have her life ruined by somebody forgetting to hold a door open for her or to offer her their seat in the same way is if she were hit by a fast moving car, so there are differences between etiquette and pure safety on the pheasant shoot.

Safety on the shoot is paramount, but it is equally true to say that it adds a great deal to the enjoyment of the sport to be out in company with people who never fail to observe the niceties of behaviour, almost going out of their way to show consideration for their companions. Anybody who has had to tolerate a jealous, greedy shooter alongside them, a man who is forever shooting his neighbour's birds before he has had a fair chance at them, will testify that it can absolutely ruin a day. And it can quickly impinge on the rules of safety if another decides to retaliate to the point where the shooting becomes a free-for-all, shooting anything and everything. But the man who calls out 'Your bird, sir' when a pheasant is passing directly between neighbours, or raises his hat to a bird that he feels is beyond his range, keeps everything in perspective.

Shooting Performance

Having just mentioned the case of a man who will raise his hat to a bird that he believes is out of range, I must immediately stress that this will not endear anybody to either the host or his keeper when they have gone to considerable expense, time and effort to show truly high and testing birds. A bird far out on the flank is one thing but a high pheasant, over the line, should not be left with the excuse that 'I'm afraid it was out of range for my old gun' or 'I am afraid I always miss those high birds', because it is your responsibility, especially when accepting an invitation, to ensure that both you and your gun are up to the task in hand. The shoots that can produce some birds which are capable of passing out of range overhead can be counted on the fingers of one, maybe two hands. You are there to shoot, rather than simply admire, the birds that host and keeper have produced.

Thankfully, however, the days have gone when a team of guests would be expected to put up an impeccable performance in terms of the number of head shot. There is a story that Lord Leicester, son of Coke of Norfolk, would bring a shoot to an early end if he felt his guests were not performing to the high standard which he set. It is said that on one occasion he actually halted the line of beaters in the very middle of a partridge drive because his guests weren't coming up to scratch. Eventually, however, his head keeper was able to persuade his lordship that the Guns' performance was as much as could be expected in the teeth of a gale, and that they could make up numbers on later drives that were less exposed to the elements.

There is another story, this time about Lord Leconfield, who ruled his shoot at Petworth with a tight rein. Come the time for his annual tenants' supper and he would not

Considerable expense, time and effort
goes into producing high, testing,
top-quality birds, and the individual should
ensure that he and his gun are up to the
challenge of shooting them.

hesitate to tell his guests that if they failed to shoot at least two hundred pheasants before lunch they could forget any notions about having grace birds to take home with them. Grace birds are the brace presented to shooting guests at the end of the day's shooting.

Such attitudes and values may seem to be long gone and, today, we insist that the accent is on quality rather than quantity, and that it is far more important for a man to behave himself well and shoot safely, and nobody would argue with these feelings. However, it would be a little bit silly to suggest that, all other things being equal, if there are two men both equal in terms of safety, consideration and behaviour, then the one who is the better performer with a gun is not most likely to receive any invitations to shoot that may become available. Particularly on those shoots where the accent is strongly on producing quality birds, shooting ability will be placed high on the list of priorities among prospective guests.

Paying and Non-Paying Guests

When talking of etiquette, behaviour and performance, the uninitiated might feel that a clear distinction can be made between paying guests, be they syndicate members or whatever, and those enjoying free hospitality. It isn't so straightforward; and this is not just because a paying guest, if he wants to be worthy of the title of 'sportsman', will behave his best and give his best performance whatever the situation and the circumstances surrounding it.

The fact is that even the paying guest must remember that shooting is a team sport, and that he therefore has duties and responsibilities towards not only the rest of the team but also the host, captain, organiser, or call him what you will. If he fails to recognise and observe these responsibilities, or, worse still, chooses to ignore his duties, it will never pass unnoticed.

An individual syndicate member will be shown, in a dozen subtle ways, that his company is no longer desired. It is true that inflation has bitten hard and that it may be difficult to find a replacement but, equally, most good shoots know of somebody who has expressed an interest in joining, or be able to find at least one 'half-gun' who will pay half the subscription and attend every second shoot, or maybe the rest of the team will simply agree to drop the offending member and share the cost, each then being allowed to invite one guest for a day. There are numerous ways to avoid keeping a man of 'the wrong sort'.

Equally, a team of guest Guns who misbehave will find that, when they seek to book a day for the following season, the host has either decided to rear fewer birds, or let off fewer days, or whatever. And, in the relatively small world of hosts and sporting agents, word quickly gets round.

Host, Captain or Organiser

On any shoot there will be one man who takes greater responsibility than his fellows. The most obvious case is the man who bears the entire financial burden and responsibility of running and organising his own shoot, and who invites non-paying guests. The fact that he will, in nine cases out of ten, send out his invitations to those who will be able to return the favour does not really matter.

Equally, he may decide to keep, say, six days for himself, and let off two days to paying guests. Except in financial terms, the situation has not changed: his word is law, he will decide when and where the drives will be undertaken and, if he says he doesn't want hen birds shot, that foxes are to be left well alone and that ground game is to be ignored, then everybody had better listen and obey.

In syndicates, things may seem rather different. However, the organiser or 'shoot captain' is likely to be the man who has found the ground, the keeper and the team

131

of Guns, as well as being the one who administers the finances and makes the decisions, and any man who takes on such a burden deserves his companions' respect. Not that he always receives it, of course. But that does not alter the fact that whether he gets a free membership, only pays a proportion of the others' subscriptions, or pays his full share and carries out his duties simply for the love of the thing, his word should remain the law. People who do not like the way he sets about things have two alternatives open to them. They can try the subtle, discreet word or, if that fails, cancel their subscriptions and move to a shoot that is more to their liking. There is nothing worse than the character who spends every moment between drives or at lunch in trying to stir up a mutiny.

The Invitation

In reality, the planning of a day's shooting will have started many months before, practically before the first egg was hatched, but, except for the host and his keeper, the shooting day starts with the arrival of an invitation or notification of the shooting days.

Sometimes the invitation may not be too specific. For example, 'Dear John, please come and shoot on 15 December, yours sincerely, James' leaves a lot to the guest's imagination. Will his useful and steady retriever be as welcome there as it is on other shoots? Are ladies welcomed as spectators? Will lunch be provided, bought in a pub, or should he bring a flask and sandwiches? How many birds are expected and, therefore, how many cartridges should be brought? Naturally, it is good sense to pack a few boxes of spares in the boot of a car, but what if stocks can't be replenished because lunch will be away from the meeting place? It is extremely embarrassing, at one extreme, to arrive with a single gun and fifty cartridges, only to find that loaders are provided, and all the rest of the team have hundreds of cartridges apiece, just as it is

Shooting with a pair of guns.

to emerge with two cartridge bags, with 100 cartridges in each, when the intention is an informal day with friends.

A telephone call will sort these things out. But how much better if the invitation had read:

Dear John,

Would you like to shoot with us at Blinkers on 15 December? We are always in need of good, steady dogs, and ladies are welcome to the shoot and for lunch, which will be at my house. We shoot with single guns. Hope to shoot in the region of 200 birds on the day. Meet at Blinkers at 9.30.

The invitation could have been written in more formal terms but, nevertheless, it is sufficient to let the guest know what is happening, where and when, and what is likely to be expected of him.

Arrival at the Shoot

On the day before the shoot, or before, you are well advised to lay out your gun, cartridges, kit and even clothes. Check that it is all there in plenty of time to make any replacements or additions that may be required.

Find out how far it is to the shoot, and allow plenty of time for any unexpected stoppages, such as to change a wheel or whatever. Even then, many experienced Shots will allow an extra twenty minutes or so. They would prefer to arrive in the close vicinity of the shoot and read or take a walk to fill in time, rather than arrive late. If they have a dog, they will give it a few minutes scamper. Otherwise, a team of labradors and spaniels can create an astounding number of puddles and piles on well kept gardens, lawns and even front-door steps.

Best of all, if you have a dog, is for it to be kept in the car until the moment when the host suggests it is time to make a move. If you like to take pride in the fact that your dog will sit quietly while all about are a pack of uncontrollables, then do so. It is very satisfying to see the tailgate up on an estate car, and two untethered gundogs waiting patiently. If they are not capable of this, keep it or them on a lead.

Get your boots, coat or whatever on. Take your gun out of its travelling case and slip it into a sleeve. Gather up your other paraphernalia, then go and stand with the other guests, close to your host. Introductions will be made, and news exchanged, but the main thing is to keep and eye and an ear on the host and be ready to gather round for 'orders of the day'.

Drawing for Places

Before or after the host has had his say about what is to be shot or left, he will go among the guests for them to draw their numbers, be it out of a hat, by short pegs with the numbers inscribed upon them, or whatever. On some shoots, the numbers are written on cards which also bear the names of the other guests and a section on which to enter the head of the various species of game shot – a nice touch for those who maintain a shooting diary and for those who have forgotten seven names within minutes of the introductions having been made.

The standard procedure is that if, say, one man has drawn number 3, that will be his peg for the first drive, numbering from the right, and he will move up two at each subsequent drive. Thus, at following drives, number 3 will move to 5, then to 7, then, assuming there are eight Guns, to 1, 3, 5, and so on. If he had drawn number 2, he would stand at 2, 4, 6, 8, 2, 4, and so on.

On most shoots, numbered pegs will have been set out, so that there is no excuse for confusion. On others, the host may choose to say something along the lines of: 'Number 1 at the side of that hedge; other Guns at about 40 yard intervals to the top of the wood', so that he can make allowances for the prevailing conditions.

There are some drives on most shoots where pheasants have a tendency to break out at the sides, or back over the beaters. The host may decide that there is a need for a walking Gun. All other things being equal, this will normally fall to one or both of the flanking Guns. Thus, if you follow the mathematics, number 1 and number 8 will be on either side of the wood, keeping in line with the beaters, and numbers 2–7 will be in the normal positions, except that number 2 will stand in number 1 position, and so on.

This may all sound rather complicated when written down on paper. However, for the Gun who is able to add two and two or subtract one from three, and who keeps his wits about him, it should not be all that difficult a task. And yet look at any shoot and you will be surprised to find graduates in mathematics, merchant bankers and men who have run rings around the Inland Revenue for years, all counting on their fingers and eventually settling for the fact that if John is on their right and Jim on their left they can't be all that wrong.

Drawing for place and moving up a set number is not used on all shoots. Sometimes, most usually where non-paying guests are involved, the host will place the Guns for each drive at his discretion. At one extreme, he may discover that a man is not entirely trustworthy and choose to keep him out on one of the flanks, where he is less likely to cause any harm or annoy his fellows. If somebody is needed to do a bit of steep walking, it will be best to send a younger, fitter member of the party, or on those inevitable occasions when a man is suffering the misery of an 'off day', with his performance well below his usual standard, he can be saved any embarrassment by being kept out of the hot spots. Equally, it may be that the host wishes to show his best birds to a particularly valued guest. However, this can go horribly wrong. One well-known British statesman tells the tale of the time when his father decided to place the guests rather than let them draw numbers. However, the birds decided that day that they would not fly as expected and, drive after drive, the host's young sons got all the shooting, while the important guest watched on. Some people could easily take that sort of thing the wrong way.

What will concern the host most of all is that he doesn't, on a draw, find that all his best Shots are standing together. It is inevitable that, among the team, there will be a few really good Shots, some not so brilliant, and one or two much poorer performers. If the best Shots are all together, say standing at 7, 8, 1 and 2 on the flanks of the best drive of the day, it could be rather a shame.

There is a little trick that was shown to me by one host. On his shoot, the draw is made with flat ivory pegs kept in a wallet. He puts the odd numbers on the right, and the evens on the left. Then, when he is offering the wallet to his best performers, he holds the wallet in his left hand, covering the even numbers. For the not-so-good performers, his right hand covers the odd numbers on the right. Thus he is not so much rigging the draw as ensuring that the moderate performer will always have a better performer on either side to help him out in tight corners.

Arrival at the First Stand

The usual form is that the shooting party, having got as close to their stands as their cars will allow, or having gathered their cross-country vehicles a little way behind the line where they will stand, disembark with their guns in their sleeves, dogs on leads, and make their way to their individual stands. Conversation should be kept to an absolute minimum. 'Game can see, and game can hear' is the watchword and any birds or vermin which might offer the chance of a shot may be turned back by loud voices.

When the peg is reached, it is time to make a decision as to where best, exactly, to stand. Sometimes a keeper will forget the needs of the shooting man and if he has

137

Pickers-up and their dogs should be in a safe position, well behind the line, but sometimes it is inevitable that they have to stand closer. Remember that, even at 100 yards or more, a stray pellet still retains enough energy to blind man or beast.

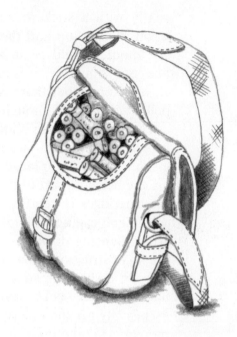

The cartridge bag should be opened,
some cartridges put into the jacket pocket,
and the cartridge bag given a shake and
placed on the ground. The lead pellets
are the heaviest part of the cartridge and
a shake will cause the cartridges to lie head
down, rim up.

placed the peg on rough or slippery ground and, three or four yards away, there is a clean patch of level ground, it is quite in order to move slightly. But no more than three or four yards.

Dogs will be considered in Chapter 12. For now, let's concentrate on the man. The first thing to do is to note the position of neighbours. This is vital for reasons of safety as well as for deciding which birds to take and which to leave. A close inspection should also be made for the presence of stops, who may be tucked away in a hedgeside, tapping gently with a stick to ensure the pheasants stay in the wood. Pickers-up and their dogs, if they know what they are about, should be in a safe position, well behind the line, but sometimes it is inevitable that they have to stand closer. Remember that, even at 100 yards or more, a stray pellet still retains enough energy to blind man or beast.

The cartridge bag should now be opened, some cartridges put into the jacket pocket, and the cartridge bag given a shake and placed on the ground. The lead pellets are the heaviest part of the cartridge and a shake will cause the cartridges to tend to lie head down, rim up.

The gun can now be taken out of its sleeve and opened. After glancing down the barrels to make sure that there are no obstructions, load the gun and settle down comfortably on a shooting stick. Some people look with disdain upon shooting sticks, saying that they should be reserved exclusively for the elderly and disabled, but others, while prepared to take their turn in walking as much as the next man, cannot see why they should stand when they can sit in comfort.

Incidentally, that reminds me of an occasion at school. I think it was during an English class but, whatever it was, we weren't paying much attention when we saw a party of Guns arriving and taking their positions. One elderly gentleman settled down on his stick, with a loader carrying his second gun standing just behind him and two immaculate labradors sitting either side and just in front. I suppose the little party might have looked rather strange, next to the posts on the First XV pitch. Anyway, it was quite some time before the first bird appeared, but it was a real screamer, straight over the old gentleman. He did not move a muscle. Then a second bird; again he did not move. At this stage, the loader took a pace forwards and peered over the shoulder of the gent, who must have been fast asleep. After a gentle shake of his shoulder, normality was resumed, and I have seldom seen such high, sporting birds killed so cleanly. We often wondered about the identity of the sleeping sportsman, but the keeper on the estate was too discreet to pass on the information, or simply had not noticed. Anyway, shooting stick or not, no sleeping on the job. There is plenty to be thinking about.

Which Birds to Shoot

Specific aspects of safety are considered in the previous chapter and so, for now, it is possible to concentrate on what birds should be shot, and which left to neighbouring Guns.

For many shooting men, the great majority in fact, the standard practice is to regard each man as having his own rectangular area, and if any bird flies into this particular section of airspace it is his, certainly to have the first crack at. This, in its most basic form, is what happens on most shoots. It has to be said, in its favour, that it has the advantages of familiarity as well as simplicity. However, there is another method and, while it may not necessarily suit each and every shoot, a study of it is certainly food for thought and may at least be the basis for adapting the standard system into a rather better one, even if only on an individual basis. It does, as it were, create the atmosphere and train of thought that is likely to create a reputation for consideration, courtesy and good sportsmanship.

It was Michael Raymont of Cornwall who first told me of this method, and I asked him to write about it for the sporting magazine of which I was owner and editor at the time. Subsequently I have seen it adopted on quite a number of pheasant shoots, and it does work very well. The basic idea is that it allows each bird to be considered on its merits and ensures that it will not be 'wasted' on one man when it could have presented a far more testing shot for one of his neighbours.

In the two accompanying diagrams, it may look fairly complicated, but if you look at each bird in turn the system becomes quite clear. Since birds will, in general, continue

141

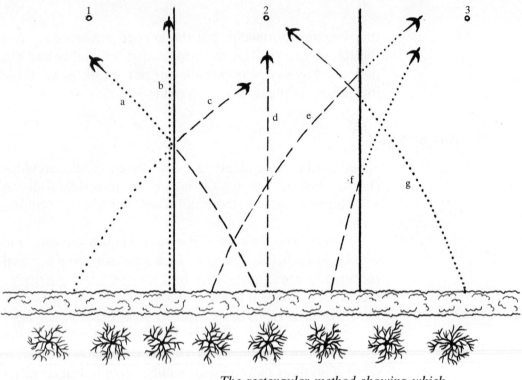

*The rectangular method showing which
bird to shoot.*

to accelerate and climb as they approach the shooting line,
it ensures that the birds are shown to their full advantage.

Bird a   This bird has risen almost directly in front of Gun
number 2 and, under the rectangular method, it remains
the bird of number 2 for that part of its flight when it is
gaining height and speed and, by the letter of the law, is
his to take until it passes into number 1's box.

By the triangular method, it is never included in number
2's area and must, therefore, be left to climb and accelerate
steadily and provide a sporting shot to number 1.

Bird b   This bird, flying directly between number 1 and
number 2, is one of those birds that always raise problems.
Whoever shoots at it first will not be censured, but the
man who passes it to his neighbour, calling 'Your bird' in

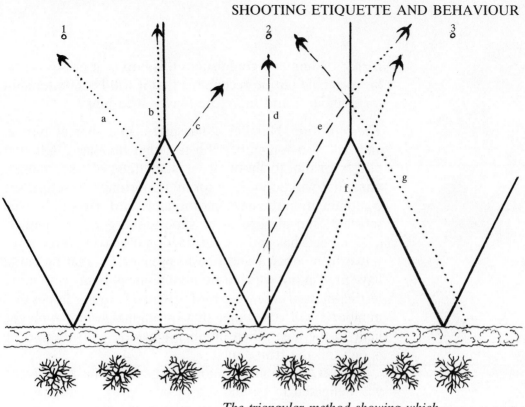

*The triangular method showing which
bird to shoot.*

a strong, clear voice, will be well on the way to gaining a reputation as a well behaved and considerate companion.

Bird c Having done the decent thing with bird a, number 2 will be expecting the compliment to be returned by number 1 with this bird.

Bird d This is the most straightforward bird of all, flying directly towards number 2, and there is never any doubt, under either system, that it is his bird.

Bird e Under the rectangular method, number 2 may shoot this bird as it passes across his front, but the triangular method ensures that it will be made available to number 3 as a fine overhead shot.

Bird f Exactly the same as bird e.

143

Bird g   Number 3 could shoot this bird as it passes across his rectangle but he recognises that it will be a better shot for number 2 and therefore leaves it to him.

The outcome   Number 1 has had a fine shot at bird a, and will also remember the fact that number 2 left that bird b for him to shoot. If he is anything of a sportsman, number 1 will be looking for an opportunity to return the compliment on the next questionable bird. He will be well satisfied, and pleased to be shooting in good company.

Number 2 has had the satisfaction of leaving three birds – two to number 3 and one to number 1 – that he could have fired at but which presented his neighbours with more testing shots. These were birds a, e and f, and he hopes that number 1 will remember that questionable bird – maybe later in the day, when number 1 has the hotspot and he is only on the fringe of it.

He was never in any doubts about taking bird d and was delighted to be allowed to take birds c and g, which were real scorchers.

Number 3, like number 1 and number 2, is well satisfied. He left bird g for number 2 Gun, but it was only a fairly low crosser for him and, in return, had first crack at e and f, high and overhead in the classic style.

Conclusion   It could be said that the diagrams show exceptional birds, except for b, which is simply the subject of common courtesy which is likely to be returned anyway, and d, of which there is no doubt. This is quite true. However, on any shooting day there will be birds such as the others which, for a variety of possible reasons, curl across the line, and it is on these birds that the rectangular method fails.

Shooting in Two Lines

It seems surprising in an age where inflation and the need to share shooting costs as widely as possible is the general rule that more shoots do not shoot in two rows. There is many a pheasant covert which in days past was considered too small for any number greater than five or six Guns, but which today may have eight or nine Guns all crammed in shoulder to shoulder.

The whys and wherefores of shooting with two lines of Guns are discussed elsewhere, but a fairly typical situation would be where the flight path of driven birds, certainly the bulk of them, is expected to be fairly narrow. There may be a front row of five Guns and three more placed some eighty or more yards behind them.

Frustration for the rear row can occur at times when the birds are flushing in ones, twos and threes, and the front row are proving themselves to be fine but inconsiderate performers. The rear row become spectators, getting very little shooting. Now, what is most annoying of all is when the rear row see that the front row are taking all the birds, including those which are only moderately testing birds for themselves but which, if left, would have had the time and space to transform into testing shots for the rear rankers.

In such situations of two rows of Guns, the front row should be careful to pick the more testing shots and, even then, leave a fair share of the birds to pass on to those waiting behind in intense expectation.

Equally, those behind should recognise their duty. It is a sad but unavoidable fact that there will always be some birds which are not shot cleanly. A bird may be seen to flinch as it is fired at by one of the front rankers, or may come on with a leg down. These are the birds that the rear row should concentrate on bringing to bag.

Keen or Just Greedy?

The general pace of modern life, which means that many men can only shoot on, say, ten days in the year and maybe less, has led in some cases to a very fine line being drawn between the keen and the plain greedy.

Where men are able to shoot on two, three or more days a week, if they are true sportsmen, it will be seen that as a rule they are careful to take only the more sporting shots, are happy to leave questionable birds to their neighbours, consider rabbits and hares with idle curiosity rather than malicious intent, and never take a shot that could be described as anything approaching dangerous. Of course, nobody would pretend that there are not certain men who shoot even five days a week and have all these faults but, on the whole, because there is always tomorrow, there is less temptation.

Compare that with the man who has to get the most out of each and every day because, quite simply, he may not be shooting again for another month. Naturally he will be keen to make the most of his chances but, just as in aspects of safety, this is no excuse for showing no consideration for his companions who, while the man feels he is just being keen, will assume that he is just plain greedy.

There is nothing at all wrong with a healthy degree of keenness, but it should be of the right type. The man who gets few opportunities to shoot should direct his enthusiasm towards making himself a valued member of the team, almost hoping for birds that will allow him to show what a considerate chap he really is. To kill a series of high birds cleanly will gain the right reputation, but that reputation will count for nothing if on the next drive a hint of greed leads to the shooting of a low bird, particularly if that bird could have been left to become a sporting proposition for a neighbour or back-row Gun.

Vermin or Predators

Whether you are of the old school which calls them vermin or the new school which refers to them as predators, you won't make friends with the keeper or score any marks with your host if you pass up an opportunity to bring a magpie, jay or carrion crow to account. If the chance arises, and it is safe, then shoot it.

Foxes are another matter entirely, and it is as well to have it established at the start of the day what is the local form. In hunting country, it is considered a cardinal sin to even raise a gun to a fox. In non-hunting country, the only sin is to miss the shot, though there is always a possibility that the host has a soft spot for foxes.

What must be avoided is to shoot at a fox when it is beyond the effective range of a weapon loaded with shot intended for pheasants. I would rather risk the wrath of host and keeper than run the risk of wounding a fox at, say, more than 25 yards. And again, always be sure that it is perfectly safe to take the shot.

Approaching Beaters

In a perfect world, there would be little risk of beaters being shot. The last birds would have risen from flushing points at least fifty yards back into the wood, and the drive would stop at that point. Equally, all that would be heard from the beaters would be the steady tap of sticks, and an occasional order from the keeper.

In the real world, few woods are planted with proper flushing points, and the progress of the beating line can be followed with the steady crescendo of whoops and war cries as they approach through the wood. About five minutes before they arrive in front of the Guns' positions, a spaniel or two will normally appear, run down the hedgeline of the wood, then disappear, happy in the knowledge that it has announced the near arrival of its master and his friends.

Whatever happens, the Guns should have a fair idea that the beaters are very close to the margin of the wood. Now, it is unlikely that anybody but the greediest of Shots will fire at a low skimming pheasant, but it is a different matter entirely if a woodcock flits out of the canopy. It may seem safe, but there is the ever-present risk of a ricochet, so no sportsman should take a shot that is not perfectly safe, well up in the air, and showing a great acreage of space between itself and the canopy of the wood.

When the beaters have taken the wood right through, the normal practice is for the keeper to give one long blast on his whistle. Whenever and wherever that whistle is blown, it signals the end of the drive.

End of the Drive

The second the signal is given for the end of the drive, the gun should be unloaded and placed back in its sleeve and there it will remain until the start of the next drive.

While you have been shooting you should have been keeping a careful mental record of the number of birds that you have shot, remembering the approximate position in which they have fallen, and paying particular attention to those birds which you have fired at and failed to kill cleanly, but which have tumbled or planed to the ground. These are likely to be runners. If a picker-up is stationed behind you, he should have it as good as in the bag, but there is no saying whether or not his attention might have been on something else.

And so, at the end of the drive, each Gun should be able to say, with a high degree of certainty, that he has for example 'Five birds down; two so close I just have to bend to pick them, one on the edge of the wood, one back in that clump of rushes and the other, I'm afraid, is a runner that planed on and into that little spinney' – or something to that effect.

The rule book states that you should now carry out the pick-up of slain birds. It says that you should probably have a word with your neighbour to ask how many birds he has to pick and then ensure that, between the two of you, you collect your combined total.

What the rule book fails to mention is one or two small incidentals, such as the fact that one beater, on emerging from the wood, picked one of your birds, the picker-up has sent forward his two labradors from behind your stand, and the dog belonging to the Gun two along from you has had its eyes glued on that runner you nicked and has already pounced upon it. Of course, this happens to everybody, so the keeper is not surprised when he asks you in passing whether you have picked all your birds to be met with the reply: 'I *think* so, but there's *maybe* a runner down which *might* not have been picked yet.'

But life is so much easier when the dogs are ruly, beaters tell you if they have picked a bird and offer to help with any others that you have still to collect, and so on and so forth. Still, time is passing by and your host and the rest of the team are waiting impatiently on the brow of a hill a quarter of a mile away, and so off you rush.

Coffee-Housing

Coffee-housing is the term used to describe the activities of those Guns who seem to believe that the sole purpose of a day's shooting is to give them ample scope to get into a little huddle and chatter to their companions, for all the world like a bunch of farmyard hens. Just like those waiters who seem to have been trained to stare fixedly three feet above their customers' heads, they are totally oblivious of any signs that the host and the rest of the shooting team are requiring their presence. This can be bad enough on any shooting day but, on a pheasant shoot, in the depths of winter, with two drives still to be fitted in before the light fades, it is utterly inexcusable.

There are plenty of opportunities to talk on a shoot, be it in the vehicles, at lunch or at the end of the day. Equally, nobody is going to say that you cannot talk at the end of a drive as you walk back to the vehicles, or to gather with your host. However, when the host and four of his guests arrive at the vehicles only to find that the three Guns on the far flank

*On any shoot, beaters are just as much a part
of the team as any man who is shooting, and they deserve
consideration and respect.*

are still discussing school fees, the merits of various cars, shot sizes or how to keep your feet warm on a snowy day, five out of eight of the team are, at best, a little unimpressed. Spare an eye and an ear to the host at all times.

Beaters, Keepers and Pickers-up

It is a sad fact that, in practically anything that is said or written on shooting etiquette and behaviour in driven shooting, no mention is made of the beaters, keepers and pickers-up. And yet on any shoot they are just as much a part of the team as any man who is shooting, and they deserve some consideration and respect.

Pickers-up are often the friends or family of one of the Guns and they spend most of the day in close proximity to the Guns, but even so there are one or two individuals who treat them with an attitude that most men would reserve for a lump of mud.

But if the pickers-up can sometimes feel their hackles rising, it is as nothing compared to the disgraceful behaviour shown to some of the beaters. What is it about some people that when they come out to the country they are so totally out of touch with reality as to believe that they have entered some medieval world populated by 'gentlemen' and forelock-pulling 'peasants'?

The simple fact is that, on practically any shoot, the modern-day beater is there because he chooses to be. Does anybody actually believe that at the present going rate of about £10 for a long, hard day, they are in it for the money?

At the End of the Day – Tipping

The shooting day may end in a number of ways, from tea in 'the big house' through to a quick drink at the local pub. Whatever the situation, grace birds, a brace for the Guns to take home with them, will be handed to them, or placed by the keeper on or in their cars.

A keeper chooses a brace of 'grace birds'
for each of the Guns at the end of
the day.

Where a keeper is employed, there may now be a scurry as
Guns, not quite sure about these things, ask each other what
tip they all feel they should give. Sometimes, but not often,
the host will tell them the amount that they should give but
usually it is left to their own discretion. It can, in fact, be
a faintly embarrassing moment for all concerned, for the
keeper as he shuffles about in the hall and for the Guns as
they search him out. Hands will be shaken at the same time
as, surreptitiously, fivers, tenners and maybe even twenties
are passed by sleight of hand. It always amazes me that a
keeper can take and slip a note into his waistcoat pocket
without even glancing at it, yet he will never drop one and
will know exactly who has given what. Otherwise, let's face
it, how could he tell his friends, as they gather round a bottle

of whisky and cans of beer provided by the host, which is a generous man whom his boss should invite back and which is a 'nouveau' who likes to throw his money about, a mean old skinflint or whatever?

It is interesting to note that some thirty years ago tips in the region of £1 for 100–200 pheasants and £2 for 300–400 birds were reckoned as being about right. Today, for those who stick to such a mathematical formula, inflation will have pushed those tips up to about £10 per 100 birds. Some areas may pay a little less and some considerably more. However, sticking with £10 per 100 birds, if they were particularly good birds, birds which the keeper had obviously put a lot of effort into, then an extra £5 would probably be in order.

However, what is most important of all is to thank the keeper personally and, whenever possible, to make an appreciative comment on his birds and the way that he has shown them.

All that remains now is to thank your host or the shoot organiser and to remember to write a short note of appreciation to him on the morrow.

10 ADVANCED SHOOTING

In discussing basic shooting techniques it may be useful to liken pheasants to targets presented at the shooting school, but clearly the appeal of pheasant shooting must go a lot deeper than that. After all, we could shoot clay pigeons at about 10p a chuck, whereas on even the most economically run shoot a pheasant will cost at least a hundred times that sum. Just how difficult a shot can top-quality pheasants present?

A Difficult Shot

A properly shown driven pheasant is one of the very hardest targets known to man. There is no need to take my word for it. In the *Badminton Magazine* of April 1905, the question 'Which is the most difficult shot?' was put to a team of outstanding game Shots of that era. Say what you like about their sporting appetites and standards, this list is made up of men who probably saw and shot more game birds in a season than the present-day shooter would manage in a lifetime. They knew exactly what they were talking about. Their answers, in condensed form, appeared in *The Shooting Week-end Book* by Eric Parker.

The Marquess of Granby: 'A genuinely "tall" pheasant, "sailing" with perfectly motionless wings, "curling" and possibly dropping as well.'

Earl de Grey, Marquess of Ripon: 'A high pheasant coming down wind with a drop and a curl.'

Lord Walsingham: 'A bird which comes *straight* over your head at a moderate height, and which for some reason (e.g. empty gun, thick wood in front) cannot be shot when approaching – you must then turn round and shoot under the bird.'

Lord Ashburton: 'A pheasant, thirty-five to forty yards away, crossing and dropping with motionless wings.'

Lord Westbury: 'Cock pheasant dropping with outstretched wings and curling away from the shooter.'

Prince Victor Duleep Singh: 'A high dropping pheasant with a wind behind and wings practically motionless.'

The Hon. A. E. Gathorne-Hardy: 'A pheasant which has come straight at you too low to shoot at in front, and which you turn round to.'

The Hon. Harry Stonor: 'A high cock pheasant flying down the line of guns with wings outstretched and motion-less.'

Major Acland Hood: 'A low partridge or pheasant on one's left.'

Mr R. H. Rimington Wilson: 'Really high pheasants in a wind and with a curl.'

Mr F. E. R. Fryer: 'A low skimming pheasant against a dark background.'

Mr R. G. Hargreaves: 'The second barrel at a flock of teal well on the wing. Ptarmigan driven round the top of the hill.'

Mr T. S. Pearson Gregory: 'Pheasants coming down a hillside and skimming with a curl below. Driven grouse in a hilly country flying in the same way.'

Mr Arthur Portman: 'High pheasants floating off a hill with no apparent movement of the wing.'

Mr H. W. Gilbey: 'A real high pheasant with a curl on.'

Of course, such brief statements leave a lot of questions unanswered, but all these names are now long gone. For example, it would be interesting to ask Lord Walsingham why he could not resist a shot at a pheasant which had passed the line, unless it was sorely hit; and one would ask much the same question of The Hon. A. E. Gathorne-Hardy. Why did Mr Fryer shoot at low-skimming pheasants against a dark background, and why were they any more difficult than grouse hugging the contours of the moor? But, leaving such thoughts aside, one brilliantly clear point emerges: fourteen out of fifteen of the most famous Shots of that era state that the most difficult shot is at a pheasant.

Let's not all start fooling ourselves into believing that they are talking about the average pheasant on an average shoot. Out of the fourteen, half of the authorities specifically mention that the pheasant must be really high, six state that the wings should be motionless, seven require it to be curling, and six say it should be dropping. You will know what they mean – the really high pheasant that has reached such a speed that there is no longer any need to beat its wings; it accelerates with a drop, tilting to curve, curl and further upset our aim. Here, surely, is the ambition of every pheasant shooter – to be able to hit such birds with anything approaching a consistent level of performance.

Let me say here and now that it is an ambition that I am still struggling to achieve. However, I think we can all take some solace from at least knowing *why* we

The really high pheasant has reached such a speed that there is no longer any need to beat its wings; it accelerates with a drop, tilting to curve, curl and further upset our aim.

continue to miss, hitting so few of these really testing birds. It is with a mixture of amusement and sympathy that I remember a fellow Gun on a shoot in Devon. He had just missed the first bird of a drive where we stood way down in the bottom of a steep-sided coomb. It had been a real rocketer, but nothing to compare with the next bird. At first, it looked as if the bird would pass over a neighbour, but then it started to drop and curl across the line. Suddenly my fellow realised that it was his bird. As he felt all eyes turning on him, and sensed the beaters coming to a brief stop to watch his aim, did he rise in elation to meet the challenge, grasp at the opportunity to make up for that first missed bird? Most certainly not. Just before he raised his gun he turned and caught my eye. With a look of abject misery he asked the question we must all have asked at one time or another: 'Why me?' As I say, I remember that moment with a mixture of amusement and sympathy – a pinch of amusement and lashings of sympathy. Perhaps if that Gun had possessed a clearer picture of what he was trying to achieve, and why he was failing, he would have been a whole lot less miserable and more prepared to welcome the chance of a second screamer. I hope so. As it was, the only possible solace for him on that drive, where the birds flew so exceptionally high and well, was that he was not the only one capable of punching holes in thin air.

Before we get totally embroiled in advanced shooting techniques with regard to pheasants, we should be quite clear in our minds that what we are talking about is, on the whole, exceptions to the rule. I have visited many pheasant shoots and, let's be honest, there are some shoots where the qualities of even a fairly high pheasant are totally unknown. Thankfully, these shoots are rare, and on the majority of shoots we will be faced with good average birds, capable of testing good average Guns, with maybe one or two drives where the pheasants fly just that little bit better, or days when the wind and sun combine to produce particularly testing birds. The fact is that there are only a handful of shoots that can *consistently* produce top-flight birds at practically every drive. Nevertheless, most of us find that at most shoots we attend there will be at least a few scorchers that test us to beyond our limits, birds that will be discussed over lunch or tea and remembered in every detail as we soak in a deep, hot bath. It is in these quiet moments that we may stop and ask ourselves why we missed it.

Talking to Experts

First, because we are only human, we will ask whether our choice of gun, cartridge and shot has been found wanting. Certainly, if you have opted for true cylinder barrels and 1 oz of No. 7 shot you may need look no further for an explanation. Such a combination is a fine choice for good, even rather better than average pheasants, but on the highest birds it simply will not do. I have spoken to many men who make it their business to snatch those high fliers down from the heavens and, time after time, they have spoken of a minimum of half choke and 1⅛ oz of shot, normally No. 7 or 7½, though some prefer No. 6 for extra hitting power at the expense of pattern density. Many of these men also choose long barrels to produce a steady, easy swing. I have seen men kill high pheasants well with 29-inch and 30-inch barrels, but I cannot recollect one outstanding performer, on these particular birds, using 25- or 26-inch tubes.

Having got our equipment sorted out – so that we have the fullest confidence in our potential, at least, to kill high, really high, birds cleanly – we can take a look at the technique and style for shooting these birds.

Basically, they pose exactly the same problems as any bird in flight. However, just like the wigeon hustling down wind like a bullet, pigeon coming into roost in a gale-torn January wood, or geese passing over the foreshore within a foot or two of being out of range, these high pheasants are able to magnify any faults that may exist in our basic technique. On an average bird, with open chokes and small shot, it will not matter too much if our aim is slightly off to the side, in front or behind; the spread of the shot will cover for our errors. However, one foot off at ten yards is four feet off at forty yards, and while the first will probably be a hit the latter will surely be a miss.

The experts talk about getting onto their birds early, studying the flight of the bird for a brief moment, and choosing the exact patch of sky – or rather the bird's position and angle in relation to themselves – where they will take the shot. You must get on the line of the bird and keep swinging.

Are Good Shots Born or Made?

Some of the best shooters, quite infuriatingly for us mere mortals, will say that they shoot by instinct or, even worse, put it down to luck. Well, I believe that men make their own luck when it comes to shooting. So what about this 'instinctive' shooting? Many writers have argued that good Shots are made, while others say they are born. My own view is that *good* Shots can be made but *great* Shots most definitely are born. The great Shots have that extra something, a fine tuning of co-ordination between hand, body and eye, that sets them apart from the common man. You could no more make a great Shot than take a boy, any boy, hurl cricket balls at him and turn him into another Viv Richards or Ian Botham. But, if that boy was reasonably able, and prepared to practise and study the style of the greats, he might at least make a county player, or certainly a very good club player. Cricket, tennis, football, shooting – you name it, it is within us all if we have the commitment to make the most of our opportunities.

In shooting, things are rather different. Nobody is forced to take part. In fact, for the majority, and particularly in driven shooting, the sport involves a heavy financial commitment. In the way of things, complete duffers tend to fall by the wayside although, of course, there is a place for all levels of performers so long as they are safe and behave with consideration for their fellows. I can think of many men who enjoy their sport enormously, are fine shooting companions and don't mind a bit of ribbing about failing to make up their share of the bag. Such characters serve as a reminder, if one is ever necessary, that shooting should never be allowed to become competitive, certainly not in the live shooting field. Those who feel the need to test or prove themselves against others should get it out of their system at clay-pigeon competitions. On live game, such behaviour is totally undesirable and reminiscent of the worst aspects of the Edwardian shooting scene. For some, it can become the ruination of their shooting.

Competence, Confidence and Concentration

Shooting is dependent upon three basic factors, the 'Three Cs' – competence, confidence and concentration. However competent we are, if we start getting angry with ourselves simply because we cannot shoot as well or better than the next person, if we allow it to become a source of anxiety, we wreck our confidence, lose our concentration, and our shooting goes to pieces, further wrecking our confidence . . . and the downward spiral continues.

Surely, then, we must all try to recognise our level of competence, always striving to do just that little bit better in order to aid our concentration – but simply for our own satisfaction rather than to prove that we are better than our companions. That way – who knows? – we may discover almost without realising it that we have in fact become better Shots than them. But who cares?

*Advanced shooting is really a mixture
of tips of the trade and the honing of basic
shooting skills to a level that allows us to
have the ability to kill the average pheasant
cleanly, consistently, and in good style.*

Advanced shooting is really a mixture of tips of the trade and the honing of basic shooting skills to a level that allows us to have the ability to kill the average pheasant cleanly, consistently, and in good style, as well as at least being able to hold our own against the occasional scorcher.

Just like building a house, we must start with the best possible foundations – crawl before we walk before we run. In our early days it is natural that we should concentrate on basic shooting techniques. We will also concentrate hard to make the rules of shooting safety and etiquette second nature. In fact, safety and etiquette are subordinated to nothing on shoots. We should always be aware that shooting is a social sport, where each individual's enjoyment is totally dependent on the behaviour of the entire team. That includes keepers and beaters as well as fellow Guns.

At best, we will allow ourselves a steady development. For example, one would not advise a middle-aged man, new to the sport and having just bought his first gun and had two or three lessons at a shooting school, to put himself down for a day's shooting at Gurston Down in Wiltshire, where they show pheasants probably equal to any in England. One man who shot there excused himself for not having performed particularly well by explaining that he was not able to spot the high birds with his binoculars, hold a gun and shoot at the same time!

It is an aid to steady shooting development that, on most shoots, the cream of the pheasants are not encountered until the tail end of the season. That is when many shoots hold their 'cocks only' days in order to maintain a well balanced breeding population, a rather unscientific way of attempting to leave only one cock to each six hens.

These battle-hardened late-season pheasants make few mistakes. Some will try to break back over the line of beaters, or out of the sides of the covert, and walking Guns can enjoy fine, testing sport. Of those that go forwards, some will have learned that flying low means they don't get shot at. The majority of those going forwards, however, will be relying on a combination of height and speed to carry them beyond the line of guns. All other things being equal, it is the highest, fastest, most athletic of the pheasant stock that have survived this long.

A Sense of Awareness

The first step in becoming a good Shot is to develop a sense of awareness. At its most basic, this means that the Shot will not arrive at his stand, take his gun from its sleeve, load it and then sit on his shooting stick with nothing on his mind but the colour of the neighbouring Gun's socks, or what they might be getting for lunch.

He should rather be remembering, or trying to picture if it is his first visit to a shoot, where the birds will appear from and where they will fly towards. He will note the position of the other Guns and any stops or pickers-up. In other words, he will be aware of what might be quite a limited patch of sky in which he will probably be making his first-barrel kills.

That sounds fairly simple, and it comes naturally with a little experience, or rather it *should* come naturally, but, to begin with, it is important to analyse some of the things it involves. In broad terms, other than the rules of safety, awareness involves the ability to estimate range, to judge how early to swing onto the first bird, to predict the likely speed of the birds and how the wind or sun may affect their flight, and even to decide which barrel to fire first. Let us look at all these in greater detail.

Estimating Range

The good Shot should be able to estimate range with a fair degree of accuracy. The shotgun is a fairly short-range weapon. I have suggested that with open chokes and light loads its range is little more than 30 yards. With tighter chokes to give a denser pattern, and a rather heavier load of shot, it may be possible to squeeze this out towards the 50-yard mark. However, all this is for naught if the man holding the gun cannot tell the difference between 30, 40 and 50 yards.

It is one thing to be able to judge horizontal range along the ground. Cricketers will quickly judge when a bird is about one pitch out from them, a little over 20 yards; if it appears to be more than two pitches away it is nearing the extremities of range for a 12-bore game gun.

However, put an object up in a clear sky and the task is very much harder. On a vertical plane, range estimation can go to pieces. It is a fact that objects look far smaller, and therefore further away, on the vertical. Consider the moon. When it is close to the horizon, it looks quite massive, far larger than when it is riding high in the sky. Also, with a clear backdrop of sky there is nothing against which to scale a bird.

It is for this very reason that so many shooting men make mistakes in judging vertical range. Time and again you will hear them describing pheasants as being out of shot when, in reality, they are no more than 60 feet up. Believe me, a pheasant flying at this height looks like a really tall bird, but the reality is that its range, overhead, is only half that of a shotgun with some choke in its barrels. One of the main contributory factors to such birds being missed is that if the Gun *thinks* the bird is out of range he will have neither the confidence nor the concentration to take the shot, however competent he may be.

For the sake of their confidence, if for nothing else, those who shoot driven pheasants should spend time discovering the height of various objects, and try to fix the scale of such heights in their mind. For example, each floor of a standard modern office block is about 10 feet tall. Therefore, obviously enough, if we choose to shoot with true-cylinder patterns and 1 oz of shot and accept that the limit of our effective range is 30 yards, we should grasp every opportunity to study the ninth storey of an office block. Picture a pheasant flying at that height – it's very tall.

Those working, visiting or living in London may care to note that Sir Ralph Payne-Gallwey, in his book *High Pheasants*, gave a number of specific examples. Nelson's Column, he states, measures 54 yards including the statue. The Duke of York's is 46 yards. Somewhere between the two lies the mark for those with fully choked guns. Street pigeons have a habit of mobbing the great Lord Nelson so, next time you are in London, take a look. Stop and think that those birds passing half-way up, which look incredibly high, are only 30 yards or thereabouts. Don't stand there looking up at them for too long. They may recognise you and your evil intent, sending down their peculiarly unpleasant version of 'pennies from heaven'.

When I studied estate management at the Royal Agricultural College, we had a large number of keen pheasant shooters on our course. In order to estimate the timber in a tree, we had to learn to estimate its height. In fact, by getting a six-foot companion to stand at the base of the tree, measuring his height against a ruler, standing well back, and then measuring the total height of the tree and multiplying, we learned to be quite accurate. If the six-footer measured 2 inches and the tree 12 inches we knew that it was 36 feet high, give or take a small amount. When we got among some really big trees – trees which, had a pheasant passed over them you would have sworn it was out of range – time and again we found that they were barely 90 feet high, often less. We learned about more than forestry when we studied estate management!

There is a great deal more to being able to judge range accurately than simply being able to say when a bird is, or isn't, in range of our gun. Good Shots always seem to have plenty of time to take their shots. They never appear hurried or flustered, even when taking a second shot at a high, fast bird. That is because they create time for themselves by taking their birds early. They seldom need to turn and take a second shot behind and therefore avoid wasting time on an exercise which, on the whole, leads only to more wounded birds. The shot taken at a pheasant when it has passed over the line and is going away is one of the most difficult of all. It is a shot that should normally be reserved for a bird that is seen to be hit but which flies on.

Take Them Early

When I am not shooting during the winter months, I often enjoy a day's beating or picking up with my dogs. Picking up, in particular, gives a marvellous opportunity to watch all sorts of Shots in action. I have noted that the best Shots will always take their first bird well in front. If they miss, they have plenty of time to take a second shot at the same bird while it is still in front or overhead. Less able performers will wait until the bird is overhead before firing their first barrel, in which case they have no time for an effective second barrel.

It is one thing to say 'take your birds early' but quite another to say how early. Unfortunately, we have to fall back on some elementary mathematics. Returning to the height of driven pheasants and estimating range, on most shoots anything over 60 feet up is considered a really tall bird. In fact that is just 20 yards, only half the effective range of a standard gun. This bird is in range when it is still 35 yards in front.

If we picture a real scorcher of a bird 30 yards up, a height of bird rarely seen on most shoots, we see that with our standard gun with a range of 40 yards we can take it while it is still 27 yards in front, though with the shorter-range combination of true-cylinder barrels and 1 oz of No. 7 shot we must wait till the bird is directly overhead.

167

What of the longer-range gun in the hands of a real crack Shot faced with the most testing of pheasants, birds that would normally be seen only on a few select shoots in the Welsh Borders and Devon, and on a handful of others in Wiltshire, a few in Scotland and some in Yorkshire? Full chokes and the right sort of cartridge might just stretch the range of our weapon out to 50 yards. Do you remember the 3–4–5 triangle? It shows us that we can take a 40-yard high bird, flying at the height of a twelve-storey office block, while it is still 30 yards in front, or to the side for that matter. But I have discussed the pros and cons of short-, medium- and long-range guns and cartridges already, so let me stick with range awareness and taking birds as early as possible. What are the real advantages of shooting early?

This leads to an awareness of the speed of a flying pheasant, the rate at which it is covering the ground. It has been calculated that a pheasant which is flying in still air will have a ground speed of about 40 m.p.h. Another way of expressing 40 m.p.h. is 60 feet per second, which is rather convenient as it means that the pheasant covers 20 yards in one second of time.

This introduces the clear advantage of taking the first shot as early as possible. If we take the first shot when the bird is still 30 yards in front and we fail to hit it, or kill it cleanly, we still have 1½ seconds to get off our second barrel before the bird has passed overhead. The same is true if we kill cleanly with the first barrel and turn our attention to a bird that has been flying alongside the first. If we had taken that first shot any later, thus failing to give ourselves as much time and space as possible, we would probably have been forced to take the second shot behind, or leave it.

How long does it take to register a hit or miss, to choose a second bird, get onto it, swing and fire? Equally, how many seconds does it take to pick up the bird for the first shot, get on *its* line, swing and fire? What space of time elapses between the start of the gun-mounting sequence and the final firing of the second barrel?

The best advice given to a man on his first visit to a moor is that he must be on his toes and take them early if he is to get his right and left from a covey of driven grouse. 'Put up your gun while they are still 60 or 70 yards in front' is the way it is often put.

Of course, nobody is suggesting that it is possible to kill the birds at 60 or 70 yards, but it takes about a second to mount, swing and fire, and in that time the approaching birds will have covered about 20–30 yards and be shot at 40 yards. If the Gun waits until the bird is in range before starting to mount his gun, he will plaster it at about 10 yards and then have no time at all for a second barrel.

Another piece of good advice from the grouse moor is, when faced with a number of birds, to choose one and stick with it. Pheasants may appear to offer more time, but we should use this to give us an edge, rather than dithering about, swopping from this bird to that. Pick the most testing, if you are a sportsman, and stick with it.

Two cock pheasants clattering up through the trees from the same flushing point, accelerating and gaining height together as they come, plumage resplendent in the low January sun. Good birds, but we reckon they will be well within range when they are still 30 yards in front. The barrels are locked onto the first choice when it is still more than 50 yards in front of the line. Take a second to mount the gun, swing through the bird and pull the trigger. Onto the second bird. His head flicks back as he crumples directly overhead.

Now and again, not too often of course, there is the evidence of a real class Shot in action. Two small piles of first- and second-barrel kills about 30 yards apart.

A strong breeze can upset all these calculations. A wind of 30 m.p.h. will accelerate the birds so that they are covering the ground at about 35 yards per second. With a following wind of this sort, if the first shot is taken with the bird 30 yards in front we have less than a second to get off a second barrel before the bird is passing overhead – less than a second to register hit or miss, swing, and take that second shot. Also, because the birds are accelerated, there are enormous advantages in mounting the gun earlier than normal for the first shot. Even those who insist on taking their shots directly overhead must see that if, say, they take $1\frac{1}{2}$ seconds to mount, swing and fire, they must be getting onto their bird, starting the mounting sequence, when the bird is still about 50 yards in front. Leave it too late with a high, fast and curling pheasant and you are making an already difficult task more difficult still.

Which Barrel First?

The development of the sporting shotgun goes well back into the days when the majority of game was shot either over dogs or by walking up. One must presume that when choke was finally introduced, allowing patterns to be tightened up for long-range shooting, the majority of shooters still shot in this fashion. Certainly the tradition was immediately established that guns should be bored to throw a fairly open pattern from the first, right, barrel, and a tighter pattern from the second, left, barrel. This is perfectly suited to shooting going-away birds which, if a covey springs or the first shot is missed, are close in when the first barrel is fired and further away for the second. However, this is far from being the best arrangement when it comes to shooting approaching driven birds. When shooting driven game, we will normally be striving to take our first shot well in front, at the greatest range, and the second shot overhead, at the shortest range.

Some modern shooters ignore these facts, or feel that they are unimportant. So for shooting driven birds they use a gun bored to throw the same pattern from both barrels. If they do not expect to visit shoots that show

170

really high pheasants consistently, they may settle for true or improved cylinders. For the most testing of birds, they might choose three-quarter or full chokes. The ideal would be to have two guns, or one gun with two sets of barrels. Either way, those who settle for the same pattern in each barrel of a double-barrelled gun need not worry about which barrel to fire first because it simply won't make any difference. Equally, the man with a selective single-trigger gun, or an over-and-under with multi-chokes, can arrange things to suit each and every situation that he encounters. But what of the great majority who settle for a double-trigger gun where the front trigger fires the right barrel, traditionally the more open?

It feels entirely natural to pull the front trigger first and then slide back onto the second, rearmost, trigger. This is the way most learn to shoot and, unless they stop to think about it, they will continue to do so. For those who are reared, as I was, very largely on going-away shots, this habit becomes ingrained. However, in driven shooting it is very poor technique.

There can be little point in arranging things so that we have one barrel best suited to taking shots at fairly close range and another for longer shots, and then to go on using them the wrong way round. Like leaving shots too late, it is making an already difficult enough task even more difficult.

The ideal solution would be for all driven shooters to accept this fact and have their guns bored the opposite way about, but, rather than listening to logic, we prefer to heed the pronouncements of gunmakers, dealers and auctioneers, who state that this would severely effect the second-hand value of the gun. So, as it seems that we all rate the gun's financial value above that of its effectiveness in the field, we have to shoot in what is an unnatural manner, or else ignore whatever advantages lie in having the ability to choose one or other barrel.

The rough shooter's target is usually
flying away from him. He is well served
by a gun which fires a fairly open pattern
from the first barrel and a tighter pattern
from the second. Not so, however, when
shooting driven game.

However, it is a great advantage if one can train oneself to shoot with either barrel. The place to do this is at the shooting school. Ask for pairs and force yourself to use the rear trigger first, over and over again. It may take several hundred cartridges and clay-pigeons before any degree of comfort is attained in swopping to either trigger at will, but the one who perseveres and practises will be able to use the gun to its full effectiveness on either going-away or approaching shots.

All that can be said is that it is a great pity that when the finest gunmakers differentiated between best-quality sidelocks for driven shooting and boxlocks for the rough shooter they didn't extend their thinking as far as the trigger arrangements. They could have stopped the ludicrous tradition of front-trigger/open-barrel on all guns, irrespective of their primary intended use.

Truly High Pheasants

What is or is not a truly high pheasant will differ from one shoot to another, and from one individual to the next. Let's face it, some people who may have shot for years have never even seen a truly high pheasant, let alone shot one. On many shoots, what is described as a 'real scorcher' will be coming over the Guns at a height of about 60 feet. It would clear the top of a modern six-storey office block. In fact that bird is flying at a height of just 20 yards, will be killed cleanly with 1 oz of shot from the most open-bored barrel and, theoretically if not practically, should not prove such a stern test to the average performer.

Every so often, certainly on most shoots that are not situated on flat ground, a drive will produce a handful of birds that are described by all present as being out of range. They look the size of starlings compared with what is shown and accepted as a good bird. And yet the person who has experience of truly high birds will judge with a fair degree of accuracy that the bird is actually flying at a little under 100 feet. Now, when you think of that in terms of modern office blocks, it is the height of a ten-storey building. However, that is still only 30 yards and, while being at the extreme limits of a combination of light load and open barrel, it is well within the capabilities of a half-choke, let alone a full-choke barrel. And there are a handful of shoots in this country where pheasants are regularly killed by the shooting experts at heights of up to 120 feet, 40 yards, the height of a twelve-storey block.

I don't suppose anybody would think it particularly clever to shoot a low crossing bird or a going-away shot at a range of 30 yards. Paced out on the ground, it seems no great distance. And rough shooters think very little of killing a fast-departing bird with their second barrel. In fact at a theoretical level, purely in terms of range, the high pheasant isn't all that testing a bird. So why is it that in practice so few of us are able to hit even the 30-yard bird with any degree of regularity? Basically, the reason that the high bird looks so high is something of an optical illusion. The solution, very largely, comes down to a case of mind over matter.

To start with the optical illusions. First, an object up in the sky looks far smaller than one seen on the horizontal plane. This is a fact. So the pheasant shooter must come to think of, and recognise, birds in terms of their appearance at vertical rather than horizontal ranges.

Next, even if the high pheasant is flying with a wind up its tail, perhaps accelerating it to 60 m.p.h., it still looks as if it is flying incredibly slowly. This is just the same as a low-flying jet fighter appearing to be so much faster than a high flying passenger liner, and yet the fighter, to fly at low altitude, is throttled right back.

When judging the speed of a flying object, it seems that we may partly think of it in terms of angular change. Take the case of two approaching pheasants, both at an angle of 45 degrees to the horizontal. If one bird is flying at a height of 25 yards, at 45 degrees it must be 25 yards in front, and at the same angle a bird at a height of 50 yards will be 50 yards in front. If we then follow the lower bird through another 45 degrees of angle it will be overhead in half the time of the higher bird. And because the angular swing has taken half the time the lower bird fools us into the impression that it is flying at twice the speed of the higher.

Sticking with the concept of angle rather than distance, a consideration of pheasants flying over the Gun at various heights and at the same speed will show that, while the required forward allowance increases with range if measured in terms of distance, it remains constant in terms of angle. The smoke-trail method of shooting clearly depends on an angular rather than a linear forward allowance being made automatically. That is, if we swing up the trail at a standard speed to overtake a bird flying at, say, 40 m.p.h., pulling the trigger as we overtake the bird, and pull out ahead of its beak, it makes no difference whatsoever whether the bird is at a height of 10, 20, 30 or 40 yards. The barrel swings through exactly the same angle in the reaction time between our brains saying 'Fire' and the cartridge being detonated, and the linear forward allowance is automatically increased by just the right amount to suit the different ranges.

That is the theory. However, it would take a very much stronger-willed person than I to look at what appears to be a tiny bird flying at minimal speed, operate the magical trick of mind over matter, and not allow the speed or the swing to fall away. For myself, as well as for the majority of successful shooters I have spoken to on this subject, it takes a very real effort to maintain the speed of swing. In fact, it feels like a real 'chuck' through the bird, to beat the optical illusion. This is better, most feel, than trying to give some fixed maintained lead of a 'field gate's length', or whatever. I have spoken elsewhere of maintained lead, but that was in conjunction with a crossing shot, a shot that gives a good impression of the speed of the bird. Try it on the apparently slow-moving high bird and it is likely to lead to a 'poking' style, where the barrel swing falls away and the bird is missed behind.

It is just as easy to be 'overimpressed' with a high bird and miss it in front. As I have said, a bird at a height of 30 yards should be recognised as the most testing that the great majority of pheasant shooters will ever fire a gun at, yet we know from the mathematics of the thing that such a bird, if flying at the average speed of 40 m.p.h.

in still air, only requires 5½ feet, less than 2 yards, of forward allowance. If we make a conscious effort to speed the swing up its smoke trail and then, in addition to this, pull two or three times the length of the pheasant out in front of it before telling our finger to pull the trigger, we shall in all probability miss the bird in front because in addition to our correct allowance we are adding a couple of extra yards. At best we will just tip the bird on the point of its beak with one or two pellets from the trailing section of the pattern. It is a case of either/or. Either you can consciously maintain the speed of your swing with a deliberate effort to apparently 'chuck' through the bird or, if your prefer or cannot make the effort, you start thinking in terms of giving the bird a couple of body lengths of lead before pulling the trigger. Having spent so much time explaining the advantages of incorporating forward allowance automatically whenever possible, there seems little point in stressing which of these two is going to bring the best results.

Droppers and Curlers

Of the outstanding game shooters of the turn of the century quoted at the beginning of this chapter, half specify high pheasants as the most difficult shots, and practically all of these add something along the lines of 'planing on set wings with a drop and a curl'. What exactly does this mean?

A pheasant, on being flushed from a wood and faced with a line of Guns, has the instinct to gain height and speed as quickly as possible. In fact height and speed are inseparable. What happens is that because the pheasant is normally capable only of fairly short but very vigorous bouts of wing flapping its primary purpose is to gain height. Having accomplished all that it can in this respect, it them simply sets its wings and begins to plane like a glider.

This is also one way of gauging in a very rough and ready fashion whether pheasants are being shown to their best advantage. As they have this habit of setting their wings when they reach terminal height, if the majority are still beating away vigorously as they cross the line of Guns the line could probably do with being moved back a bit. It is something of a juggling act, however, because from the moment they start to plane they are beginning to lose height – although, of course, they are accelerating.

Therefore it is not so much a case of planing on set wings *or* dropping but a little of both. If birds have set their wings and started to plane just in front of the line of Guns, they are at their maximum height and approaching maximum velocity as they accelerate down. This is assuming that they are flying over a flat field. If the birds are flushed over a valley, with the Guns in the bottom, although in terms of height above sea level they drop when they start to plane, if the valley falls away quite quickly they will in fact be gaining height or certainly vertical range relative to the ground since they plane at a fairly shallow angle. What's more, when these pheasants cross the Guns they will be at maximum speed. No wonder steep-sided valleys are considered such an asset on any pheasant shoot!

The important thing to remember is that while a pheasant planing on set wings may appear to be making very little effort it has set its wings only because they cannot carry it any faster.

Equally, pheasants do not always fly in a straight line. Sometimes they fly with a curl. On a day of really strong winds, their own flight pattern may carry them forwards at 40 m.p.h. but a 40 m.p.h. side-wind will carry them sideways at exactly the same rate, for every yard of forward movement the bird will also slip a yard to the side. This means that such a bird will require as much lateral allowance as forward allowance, and the gun will have to be swung on a line well outside the wingtip on the inside of the curve.

It doesn't need a wind to give pheasants a sideways curl. Take the example of pheasants flushed out over a valley. They may have been feeding in a game crop and been flushed from there, but the wood in which they were released and have been hand-fed and which they regard as home is not straight across the valley but quite some way down it. In such a case, the pheasants will fly out and then start to curl across the line of Guns towards their home wood. The curl may not be as strong as in the case of a gale blowing across their flight paths but it is there none the less and experienced Shots will note it and swing through the wingtip on the inside of the curl to ensure that the pattern of shot will be centred, rather than off to the side of the bird.

The great thing is to maintain a sense of awareness, to recognise that a bird which has started to plane and drop on set wings is as fast as ever it is likely to be and therefore requires an extra effort in the swing. Also, to take a second to study the bird's flight and note the need to make any additional and lateral allowances for a sideways slip. One might think that shooting high pheasants wasn't difficult enough already!

11 TRAINING A DOG

Many people have no desire to own and work their own dog. They are happy to concentrate on their shooting. For others, shooting is not the same thing without a good dog. Their canine companion becomes an essential ingredient of any shooting day.

The following notes cannot be described as anything like a full appreciation of the subject of a dog for the pheasant shooter. On the other hand, it is all too easy to make mountains out of molehills, and end up with something that sounds far more complicated than it ever needs to be. At the end of the day, all that the average pheasant shooter requires is a working companion, not a performing seal. The only questions are which breed, how to choose a puppy, how to train it, and then how to handle the mature dog in the shooting field.

Breed

Two main types of gundog are seen on a pheasant shoot. These are spaniels and retrievers, or, to be more specific and in nine cases out of ten, English springer spaniels or labradors.

For those who intend to walk as well as stand, there is everything to be said for spaniels. Their role is to hunt and

179

flush game and then, when it has been shot, to retrieve it. However, by the nature of their work, they are very busy little dogs. They are always pushing at the thin dividing-line between fast and efficient hunting and simply running riot. It can often take the firm hand of an experienced trainer and handler to set and keep them on the right paths, particularly those specimens from highly tuned stock. Ask a spaniel to sit

For those who intend to walk as well as stand, there is everything to be said for spaniels. Their role is to hunt and flush game and then, when it has been shot, to retrieve it.

and wait throughout a long pheasant drive, when the beaters and their spaniels seem to be having all the fun, and, if it is any good, every muscle of its body is itching to go. It may start to whine. From the tip of its shivering nose to the end of its twitching tail it shows that for spaniels of the right sort retrieving fallen game that they haven't hunted and flushed themselves is like potatoes without the meat and sauce.

It has taken me a few attempts with spaniels to get the sort of dog I want – one as keen as mustard but with an eye and an ear for my signals and commands and one which is prepared, just as long as I don't expect it to do so too often, to sit and wait at a peg on the pheasant shoot without being tethered, and to rest quietly in a hide beside a flight pond. But I had trained a few labradors before I even considered trying a spaniel and, even then, as I have said, my first two were very definitely not for appearing in company.

The labrador, on the other hand, as a first dog, has everything to recommend it, particularly to the man who will stand and wait for the game to come to him rather than walking after it. Besides being excellent family and house dogs, having the sort of placid temperaments, in most cases, that makes them first choice as guide-dogs to the blind, they are very simple to train and handle. Sure, they never make outstanding hunters, or very rarely so, but they more than make up for this in their principal role, which is as retrievers of dead or wounded game over land or in water. Choose the right sort of labrador pup, from proven working parents, and it will virtually train itself.

Apart from when it is sitting and waiting at a drive or actually retrieving, the labrador you choose will spend most of its working time in walking to heel. Experience seems to suggest that close heel-keeping may be an inherited trait. If you are choosing a pup from a bitch that has not been seen in the field, it is certainly a good idea to ask to see her, and ask the breeder to walk her about fifty yards and back again, in order to see how she behaves in this respect. A bitch that does well, without repetitive orders, at least carries the hint that her progeny should be fairly biddable and controllable.

Dog or Bitch?

The first question on many people's minds when choosing a pup is whether to go for a dog or bitch. The general rule is that the bitch should be more placid and less prone to wander. However, because she comes into heat every six months, and in that state cannot be taken into the shooting field to upset all the dogs, she will not necessarily be first choice.

Personally, I tend to prefer dogs. Maybe their temperament suits me better. I have not found them more prone to wander than bitches and, the labrador's temperament being what it is, there are no problems except that some dogs will develop a 'cock of the walk' attitude, showing aggressive tendencies towards their own kind. I have a dog like this myself. He was always the perfect gentleman until about his fifth season; then, even if he didn't start fights, he finished one or two caused by his arrogant attitude. Having been a constant companion, I couldn't bring myself to have him castrated as so many people advised but decided that he would only come out when I was shooting alone. He revels in water work and, being a big, strong dog, is something of a specialist in long-distance retrieves on duck and geese. He is also a marvellous guard dog for a family living in a country home.

Ironically, some two years after he was confined to solitary outings he ripped his scrotum while jumping a hedge. The wound became infected, flesh had to be cut away, and at the end of the day the vet decided to remove his testicles. I thought this might mean he could enjoy a few more seasons of shooting in company. His bark never changed a note, however, still rumbling up from his deep chest into a thunderous roar, and his attitude to other dogs did not seem to change one jot. Then, slowly, he became more and more placid. Today, I can take him anywhere. He is as courageous as ever. Only the aggression has gone.

Puppy or Trained Dog?

Many will say that they have neither the time nor the experience to train a labrador, let alone a spaniel. Therefore, they may decide to buy a trained dog, probably with one season's experience already behind it.

I have no doubt that in some cases this can work quite well. However, I am always left wondering how, if they haven't the experience to train a pup, they expect to manage with a mature dog. A working gundog is not a robot, responding to the pressing of buttons. Give a really excellent and useful dog to an inexperienced handler and it can be ruined in double-quick time. It takes a great deal of compassion and consideration from even an experienced person to ensure that a dog which is new to him makes the transition from one master to another smoothly. The sad fact is that being able to afford to buy a racehorse doesn't mean that you can ride it to the winning post. Many people simply fail to understand the canine brain. Told one week that the dog comes back to a whistle, next week they will be shouting 'Will you come back here you bloody dog? Dammit, come back here right now!' – which has about as much effect as reading out from 45 to 57 off a Chinese menu.

As long as experienced dogs are sold to inexperienced owners, somebody, somewhere, will be heard moaning that 'Old John Smith sold me this mutt, told me it was a really first-class animal, but it won't even sit when it is told.' Having been told by Old John Smith that the dog has been trained to drop to the command 'Hup', the new owner turns to the dog cringing by his side and says 'Come on you flaming animal, sit down when you are told', just to show the assembled party that what he says is correct.

Really, somebody should open kennels for men as well as dogs, and train them together! In the meantime, I hope the notes on handling a trained dog in the field, which appear at the end of this chapter, may at least go some way to avoid having a good dog ruined and to allow the proud owner who has invested a great deal of money to realise something of its potential.

On the other hand, give a puppy to a man who is willing to find time to give to it and, if that puppy is a labrador of the right sort, from good working stock, the man's experience will grow with the dog's stature. He will be training himself at the same time as he is training the pup, and he will quickly come to realise what he can or cannot expect. All it takes, at this level, is for the man to stay just one step ahead.

Kennel or House Dog?

A pup should be allowed to enjoy his early days to the full. Up to the age of six months, it is always best if he spends as much time as possible in the house with his new family. If he is to become a family pet as well as a working gundog, he will probably spend all his time in the house.

If there are children, it is important to explain that the pup is not a toy. They should be aware that under no circumstances should a stick be thrown for the pup to fetch. A pup at one end of a stick and a child at the other, having a tug of war, or snatching the stick away from the pup, is a sure way to ruin his potential.

The advantage of the pup being kennelled, certainly after serious training has been started at the age of about six months, is that even when he is not receiving the full attention of the trainer or a responsible member of the family he is denied the possibility of roaming about and picking up bad habits. And when a kennelled pup is taken out of the kennel for a training session, it will be the highlight of his day and he will be all the more keen for that.

The Programme

The pup will start learning a few very basic things from the day it arrives at its new home. However, serious training should not be contemplated until he is at least six months.

Steady, unhurried development is the way to transform a pup into the right sort of dog. It is wrong to expect too much, and nothing should be rushed. As a rough guide, initial obedience training, which must be thoroughly mastered, will take about three months. Then a start can be made on more specialist aspects of gundog work. Allowing another three months to polish the pup's natural retrieving abilities and give him experience in jumping walls, and so on, he should make the transition from training area to the shooting field at the age of about twelve months.

Training doesn't stop on the day of the pup's first shoot. A close eye must be kept on him throughout his first season. In fact, many owners will leave a youngster at home when they are shooting themselves and give the dog experience under their close attention by volunteering to pick up at other shoots.

*Many gundogs' first introduction to
live game is on wild duck in September,
when the dog is about one year old.*

All this has a bearing on the pup's ideal birthday. As he is ready to start his shooting experience at the age of twelve months or thereabouts, it is obvious that the autumn-born pup has great advantages. Personally, I like a pup to have been born in August or September. He will be ready to start serious training at just the right time, in the spring when the days begin to lengthen and working people can make the most of the light evenings. As the need to intensify his training grows, there are the even longer summer evenings and, if all goes according to plan, he is ready to retrieve 'the real thing' a year after his birth in early September. This might be a day's picking up on a small grouse moor – nothing too heavy – and the pup will accompany me to shoot the first of the duck and some rabbits around the farms where I can shoot. However, if things have taken longer than expected, there are still another two months before pheasant shooting is really under way.

The argument for a spring-born pup is that it has the long days of summer to grow and develop. However, while this might be true of wild animals raised on a hillside, it is hardly true of a gundog pup raised in a centrally heated house or warm kennel. The transition of a spring-born pup comes to a dead stop one year later when, ready to make the move to the shooting field, he has to hang about and pick up bad habits for many months. Equally, there is the strain of trying to find time to train a pup in the winter months when we are all going to and returning from work in the dark.

Little and Often

A pup's brain is small, and its ability to concentrate and learn is extremely limited in terms of time. Trying to train just at weekends is wellnigh impossible. What he needs is about twenty minutes each day, to include five minutes of scampering about and enjoying himself. Even in that short time, he can lose interest and concentration. Never push things because all that is likely to happen is that the trainer will lose his patience, and the pup his trust. Have a romp instead, because there is always tomorrow and next week.

Retrieving

Because it will not be mentioned again for quite some time, it is important to stress that in the early stages repetitive retrieves over short grass have the very adverse effect of teaching a pup to hunt with his eyes, rather than his nose. Equally, you run the risk of boring the pup.

Naturally, the new owner will be keen to see that his pup has the right instincts but, once the pup has shown that it is prepared to carry a glove, a knotted handkerchief or whatever, it is always best to resist the nearly overwhelming desire to be always throwing something for the pup to fetch. Plenty of time for that later on.

The First Lesson: Sit

Having said that the first lesson is to teach the pup to sit, there is, of course, one lesson and command which is even more fundamental. It will probably be used in the first twenty minutes of getting the pup home. It is 'No', which should be said in a deep, gruff and admonishing tone.

Other than that, we need to lay the foundations of recognition for the verbal and hand signals that convey to the pup that he is required to stop what he is doing and sit down. Together, the 'No' and 'Sit' commands are the essential basics of dog training. Some trainers and handlers prefer the traditional 'Hup' – indeed, I do myself – but for present purposes here I shall use 'Sit'.

The accepted hand signal to accompany the command is a raised hand, rather like a policeman stopping traffic. Because a gun is normally carried in the right hand, all hand signals are given with the left.

Most training is carried out to encourage or utilise the natural instincts of the dog, rather than forcing it to do something that it cannot understand. For this reason, the 'Sit' command is best taught through an association of actions, sounds and signals.

Having given the pup a week or so to settle into his new environment, the trainer stands with the pup's bowl held at waist level in his right hand. The pup will scamper about, not knowing why he is not getting his food immediately. After a while, the pup will be thoroughly fed up and, in order to survey the remnants of a happy life where food was freely available, he will sit down. As he does so, the trainer raises his left hand and says 'Sit', putting down the bowl of food at the same time. The seeds of association of ideas have been sown.

At the next meal time, and the next and the next, the pup will remain apparently unaware of what is expected.

The trainer must be patient, standing and waiting for many minutes if necessary, but each time the pup sits, sees the signal and hears the order and is rewarded with food, the stronger the association grows. It may take weeks, even months, for the penny to finally drop but, after that, it will be a race for the trainer to get out the command and give his signal before the pup has dropped to his haunches. But, to avoid rushing anything, only at meal times at this early stage.

Walking to Heel

As soon as the pup is taken out and about, after he has had his injections from the vet, there will be times when he must be kept under control. He must become accustomed to walking on a lead. The best lead of all is a strap with a handle at one end and a D-ring at the other, to form a noose.

When the pup has matured into a working gundog, as a retriever his place will be on his owner's left side, with the dog's nose about level with his knee. Again, this is because the gun is normally carried in the right hand.

There is likely to be some small difficulty in introducing the lead to the pup. He may refuse to budge or panic at the restriction. Confidence must be built. The trainer should get down on his knees and play with the pup, then try to get him to come on a few paces before playing some more, and so on. Make a game of it and quite soon the pup will be trotting along quite happily.

When the pup gets to about five months, the degree of control must be increased. This will avoid the formation of bad habits.

If the pup rushes ahead, the trainer gives the command 'Heel' and jerks the pup back into the correct position alongside and on the left. If the pup lags behind, the order is repeated and the pup is jerked forwards. The pup should never be dragged but be positively jerked into the correct position – not too hard but sufficient to let the pup know what the score is.

With a pup chosen from the right sort of stock, a close-heel-keeping mother, there should be few problems. However, if the pup shows real signs of confusion and panic the jerking should not be overdone. It is better to leave things be for a few days, and avoid making the puppy shy of walking at heel.

Come Here

From its earliest days, the pup should be getting used to its name. The trainer will take him out into the garden and, being an inquisitive little creature, the pup will wander off to investigate. But he still feels very vulnerable. He needs both the comfort and the presence of the trainer for reassurance.

If the trainer squats down and calls the pup's name, the pup should come waddling over to have his ears tickled. If he just looks, the trainer can jump up and run away. If there is a good relationship between trainer and pup, the pup will not be left behind. The trainer will trot away slowly, calling the pup's name, and when the pup catches up, the trainer will make a big fuss of him. It should not be done more than once or twice a day or else the pup, if he is bright and has an independent streak, may quickly realise that the trainer is really running to nowhere. And, when it comes rushing up for cuddles and rough and tumble, the initial fear of being left behind is reinforced with pleasure.

When the pup is about four months old, maybe a little later, it is time to introduce the recall signal. Everything is done as before except that as the pup starts to run back to the trainer the trainer blows two short peeps on a whistle. After a week or so of daily sessions with name and whistle together, the name can be dropped and the whistle alone will be enough to stimulate a fleeting sense of insecurity, which is dissolved with the trainer's reassurance after the pup has rushed up to him. If the pup seems confused or stubborn the trainer will, as before, jump up and run away. Make it all a game and keep the pup's tail wagging.

Introduction to Gunfire

Few dogs were ever born incurably gun-shy; many have been made gun-shy. When the pup is very young, the trainer may clap his hands, just once and not too close, while the pup is eating his meal. When the pup has got thoroughly used to this noise, the trainer may bang a tin plate with a piece of stick.

A little later, the pup can be fed outside and, while he is eating, a single shot can be fired from a starting-pistol at a range of 20 yards. Of course, if the trainer happens to live in a built-up area he should let the neighbours know what he is doing or he may be visited by the boys in blue, come to introduce their own variety of working dog to the seat of the trainer's pants.

Each day, the trainer comes a little closer to the pup until, after a fortnight, the pup is happily eating while a shot is fired at about 10 yards.

Later, when the pup has started into serious training, at an age of about seven or eight months, much the same method is used to introduce him to the sound of a shotgun. The trainer stays with the pup while a companion fires a shot at about 20 yards range, then at about 15 yards, and so on. Of course, if the pup shows any signs of anxiety, he is quickly reassured by the trainer.

Introduction to Water

When the pup is about six months old, whenever the warmer weather starts, he can be introduced to water. Even if there are no definite plans to use the pup for retrieving duck in his later years, many pheasant shoots have rivers and streams running through them. Anyway, if a Gun is invited to stay on at a flight pond after the pheasant shoot, he and his dog will look very silly if the dog shows a reluctance to swim.

Probably the best way to introduce a pup to water is to take him in the company of an experienced dog and with the trainer wearing waders. The trainer walks in at a gently shelving point in a pool or river, somewhere without too strong a current, and encourages the pup to follow. If this is not sufficient, the sight of the older dog swimming should be enough. If all else fails, the pup can be carried out and gently lowered into the water, being reassured all the time.

With nearly all the labradors I have owned, the problem has not been getting them into the water. It has been getting them out of it.

Jumping Obstacles

I have seen gundog manuals that devote an entire chapter to training a dog to jump over a fence or wall. At the end of the day, experience is the thing. If you take a pup on country walks, it will be learning at an early age how to scramble over objects in its path. Naturally, the pup should not be allowed to jump anything high, such as a wall, as this may damage his legs before they are fully developed. As with most things, jumping is just a natural progression to higher and higher obstacles.

Barbed wire is an absolute menace and dogs can gash themselves badly on it. Be very careful in this respect.

Transition to Serious Training

As the trainer takes his pup into the second and more serious aspects of obedience training, he should be very wary of rushing anything. He should remember that what happens in the next few months will be reflected in possibly ten seasons of the dog's working life. It simply does not matter whether the pup is ready for the first shoot of the coming season. Great patience must be shown at all times. An increasing measure of control is being built up, but the pup must be kept happy, tail wagging, at all times.

Sit and Stay

The trainer puts the pup on his lead, walks him along, then stops and commands 'Sit' at the same time as giving his raised hand signal. Because the pup has built up such a strong association of ideas through his meal times, he should drop to his haunches immediately. However, the concept that is now to be introduced is that once he has sat down he must stay there until he is released.

The chances are that the pup will stand again almost as soon as he has sat down. The trainer lowers his hand and pushes down on the pup's haunches, holding them down if necessary, and repeats the command 'Sit'. The pup is kept sitting for at least ten seconds. Whenever he stands, the order is repeated and he is gently but firmly put back into position. Soon the pup will realise what is required.

From that time on, whenever the pup is commanded to sit, he should never be allowed to move for at least ten seconds. He will be learning, at the same time, to sit and wait for his meal to be given to him. The trainer will tell the pup to sit, and slowly lower the bowl to the floor. If the pup moves forwards, as he will, the bowl is lifted and the command repeated. In a week or so, it will be possible to put the bowl down and make the pup wait for ever longer periods before he is told to eat. This way, the pup is not only learning to sit and stay, but also to continue doing it in the face of strong temptation. This is excellent grounding for the day when the mature dog is expected to ignore a pheasant falling within a few feet of where he is sitting, rather than rushing to retrieve before he has been given permission.

Once, when shooting at a field trial, I saw a young labrador eliminated because it took *one* step towards a bird that had fallen and bounced in a flurry of feathers not six feet from where it was sitting with its handler.

Harsh judgement, you may say, but the judge felt that it showed signs that the dog was not under perfect control.

Now is the time to introduce the whistle signal. The hand is raised, the verbal command 'Sit' is given and, as the dog's haunches drop, a single long blast is blown on the whistle. If the pup jumps up, he is pushed down on his haunches and the signal, command and whistle blast are repeated. The whistle should be a good long blast so that the pup quickly comes to differentiate between it and the two short peeps of the recall signal.

After the pup has got used to the combination of signal, command and whistle, after a week or two the command can be dropped. There should be little problem in getting the pup to sit to signal and whistle alone.

Stop and Sit

So far, all the sitting lessons will have been done with the pup on the lead, or when the trainer has his full attention at meal times. It is time, however, to cut the cords of close control and to start the process of getting the pup to stop and sit wherever he is and whatever he is doing. This is a vital accomplishment for a working dog. Whatever he does wrong, whenever he may be running the wrong way or into danger, he can be stopped immediately.

The pup will be taken on to some grassy area and waved away to play. As he passes about 10 yards from the trainer, the trainer raises his hand and gives a long blast on the whistle. Rather than actually sitting, the pup may either stop and stand or else approach the trainer. In either case, the trainer will stamp his foot angrily, take a pace forward and repeat the signal and whistle blast. If even this fails, the pup will be approached and pushed firmly into position. The pup is kept sitting for a minimum of ten seconds, then waved off again.

With a little perseverance, the message sinks in. After that, on subsequent days, all that is necessary is to increase the range until the pup will sit without hesitation at 40 or 50 yards. At this range the temptation when the pup has been sitting for ten seconds or more is for the trainer to take the lazy option and simply give two short peeps on his whistle, bringing the pup to him. However, this may lead to the pup anticipating the recall whistle and making him unsteady so at least three times out of every four, after waiting, the trainer should walk to the pup before releasing him. If the pup moves, he will be caught by the scruff of the neck and taken back to his original position and reseated.

Having mastered this, it will be a simple matter for the trainer to order the pup to sit before walking off 50 yards, waiting a little while, and then walking back. Again, if the pup moves, he must be dragged back and put into his original position. On this there can be no compromise.

The Long Stand

At the school which I attended, a navel cadet school, there was a fine example of schoolboy humour at its lowest. A new boy would be sent off to the dock with the instruction to ask one of the older cadets for a long stand. Having made his request, the older cadet would tell him, in impatient tones, that he was very busy and that the boy would have to wait for a few minutes until he was free. It was possible to keep some boys hanging about for as much as an hour before telling them that they had already had their 'long stand'.

As may be imagined, this was all very silly and extremely boring. That is worth remembering because the time has come to start introducing the pup to the canine equivalent of 'the long stand'. And, if we take the boredom to extremes with a young pup, we run the risk of making him unsteady and fidgety.

It has been stated that when told to sit the pup should be kept down for at least ten seconds. When the pup has matured, however, he is going to be expected to sit patiently for very much greater periods, through the course of a long pheasant drive for example. Therefore, over the coming months, every three or four days, just once to stop the pup getting too bored, keep him sitting for a fairly long period. For the two occasions in the first week this need only be a couple of minutes. The next week it may be a little longer. After a month or two, just once or twice a week, the pup will be expected to sit for about twenty minutes as the trainer watches television, potters in the garden, or washes the dishes. If during this time the pup moves off, as always he is dragged back by the scruff and repositioned.

The Disappearing Trick

To reinforce in the pup's mind that he must sit and stay until Judgement Day if necessary, he should now get used to staying while the trainer disappears from sight. The pup is sat down about 20 yards from a bush. The trainer walks to the bush and then behind it. If the dog seeks to follow, he is dragged back, the whistle and hand signal are repeated, and the trainer goes off and disappears again. Perseverance is the thing. After a few of these sessions, gradually extending distance and time, it will become possible to walk 75 yards, disappear for five minutes, reappear, and then walk back to the pup.

Walking to Heel

Greater control must be exerted in terms of walking to heel because, until now, the pup has only had to do this when walking on his lead. It is time to take it off, and the best place to do this is in a fairly narrow alley or lane with a wall or hedge on either side.

The trainer sits the pup and removes his lead. After waiting a few seconds, he gives the command 'Heel' and walks on.

The trainer is carrying a rolled up newspaper and, if the pup seeks to push ahead of its correct position, nose in line with the trainer's left knee, he gets a light tap on the nose, just enough to ease him back. If he lags behind he is taken by the scruff and dragged on for a few paces. In either case the 'Heel' command is repeated. A pup which has had plenty of experience on the lead will quickly catch on to what is required.

It is at this stage that a signal and sign can be introduced: a snap of the fingers and pointing at the left heel as the command is given. Again, after a few weeks, it should be possible to drop the verbal command and, when out for a walk, to bring the pup in from short range by snapping the fingers and pointing at the heel.

Thus there are now two 'Come here' commands: two short peeps on the whistle at long range and a snap of the fingers at shorter ranges, up to a few yards.

Test of Obedience

A small test of obedience, at this stage, is required to assure the trainer that his pup has thoroughly grasped the foundations of obedience training. If the pup fails the test, it is really his trainer's fault. No further training can be considered until the pup has passed with flying colours on two consecutive days. In order to make the test a little bit more difficult, no verbal commands should be given. It is a great advantage, particularly when working at long range, to be able to control a mature dog by whistle and signal alone. And it looks very pretty.

The pup is taken into a field on the lead. He is made to sit while the lead is removed and then, to a click of the fingers, he is walked at heel around the field. Arriving back at the original point, he is ordered to sit.

The trainer then walks off diagonally across the field. He squats down against the wall or hedge, which effectively makes him disappear, and after a minute or more he walks back. The pup is kept sitting for another minute, and then waved off to play. When the pup is about 30 yards from the handler, he is stopped and sat down with the combination of whistle and hand signal. The trainer waits half a minute, then walks straight up to and beyond the pup, stopping when he is, again, about 30 yards away, and after a minute calls up the pup with two peeps on his whistle. And what a joyous scene will follow if the pup has passed with flying colours!

Counsel of Perfection

If this test sounds like a counsel of perfection, well, it is meant to be. I have to admit that it is very much a case of do as I say, rather than do as I do. My own dogs would have a very good laugh to themselves if they could read all that I have been saying. However, we learn from our mistakes, and what I am saying is how I shall approach the training of my retrievers in the future, rather than discussing the mistakes of the past! A long succession of pups turned workers have made me realise that it is this basic obedience training, stuff that can be learned at a local class intended for family pets, which is the be-all and end-all of gundog training.

So far I have said nothing about the pup learning through its own experience. In fact, experience is very largely the downfall of obedience training, rather than its ally. If certain standards of control cannot be achieved when the pup has nothing else on its mind, what chances are there of stopping it when it has become a mature dog, has a sneaking suspicion that it knows what is best, and is going hell for leather after a runner that is leading it straight into the wood where a hundred pheasants are assembled, ready and waiting for another drive?

That is why I suggest that, although the emphasis is now very much on harnessing natural hunting instincts and developing them through experience for the pup, the obedience test should be repeated at least once a fortnight, and when standards are seen to slip all other training should cease until things are set back on the right course by brushing up the basics.

Retrieving

The trainer's aim is to produce a mature dog that will wait patiently at the fall of game, then retrieve it with a maximum efficiency in the minimum time. In order to achieve this, one thing must be encouraged and another avoided. What needs to be encouraged is the pup's ability to use its nose and think for itself. What must be avoided is boredom induced by monotonous, over-simple, short-range retrieves. That is why retrieving has been avoided so far. The pup should come to it fresh and eager.

The trainer will need at least three dummies. Personally, I make two of these from old washing-up bottles with the tops cut off. The bottle is filled with sand to weigh about 1½ lb, and the end plugged with a plastic bag, the whole thing wrapped in some old material – hessian is ideal – and then it is stuffed inside an old sock. Some people suggest using a bright colour. When you are trying to teach a pup to use its nose, why encourage it to use its eyes? Far better to use a shade of green or brown.

The other dummy is exactly the same except that it is stuffed with wood shavings to make it float. This is for teaching the pup to retrieve both from and across water.

Introduction to Retrieving

Any labrador worthy of the name should retrieve a dummy. If necessary, the trainer will let his pup at least sniff at it. Then, having sat the puppy down, he will walk a few paces from him and throw the dummy away behind himself. Pup, trainer and dummy are therefore all in a straight line, and if the pup 'runs in' to the fall of the dummy he can be grabbed en route and dragged back to his original position.

If the pup doesn't move, and he shouldn't if he has passed his obedience test, the trainer walks back to his side, waits ten seconds, then waves him forwards with the command 'Fetch'. If the pup is confused, the trainer encourages him on to the dummy.

It is an instinct with labradors to pick things up. The instant his mouth has closed round the dummy, the recall signal is given, two peeps, and the trainer may squat or run away to encourage the pup to come tearing up to him.

The trainer will be in no great rush, once the pup has come up, to take the dummy. There is nothing worse than a pup which drops its retrieves. Encourage the pup to hold the dummy, tickling his chin, then gently roll it down and out of his mouth.

Retrieving from Cover

That is the first retrieve over, and it will have been done on fairly short grass. It is also the last dummy retrieve which should be done on short grass. From now on, the dummy will always be thrown into cover. Indeed, right through the dog's first seasons, he should never be sent to retrieve any game that is lying in plain view, as this only serves to encourage him to retrieve with his eyes rather than with his nose. Once a dog starts retrieving with his head up he will be ruined for game finding.

The process is just as before, except that the dummy is thrown into longish grass, light scrub, or whatever.

To avoid any hint of unsteadiness, even now the pup should only be allowed to recover at most two out of three dummies that it has seen thrown. The other one should be picked by the trainer as a reminder that the pup hasn't the right to retrieve everything it sees fall. The only exception to this general rule that I can think off is when the floating dummy is thrown on deep water. And always make the pup wait for at least a minute before it is sent to retrieve, whatever the situation.

Multiple Retrieves

The next thing is to sit the pup down and throw two dummies, with a gap of about ten seconds between each. When sent out, the pup will probably fetch the last dummy to be thrown but forget the first one. But the trainer must remember where it is and, encouraging the pup, lead him to the fall.

This builds confidence and memory, and after a few sessions the pup should not hesitate much before rushing back out to search for the other dummy. He won't remember where it has gone, not in the early stages while his 'memory' is still developing, but be patient and he will hunt it out with his supersensitive nose.

Blind Retrieves

When out shooting, there are many occasions when a Gun and his dog are asked to pick a bird for a neighbour that neither has seen fall. Directions may be vague – 'Somewhere in that patch of scrub.'

The dog must have faith that when his owner says so there really is something to be fetched, and obviously he must have the ability to go out and find it.

To prepare for this, the trainer will leave his pup in the car, or house, or wherever – anywhere where the pup cannot see what the trainer is doing. The trainer then walks off to a patch of cover, throws in a dummy, and goes back and fetches the pup. The pup will be walked at heel up to the cover, ordered to sit for a few seconds, then ordered to 'Fetch' as the trainer waves his hand at the cover.

The pup will be totally confused. He will probably have to be encouraged and led forwards to where the dummy is lying. However, once this has been done a few times his confidence will grow and he will soon be tearing off on command to find what is missing. This can be taken a step further when two dummies are thrown blind into cover.

After a few sessions of this, the pup's experience is really forging ahead. The trainer will be delighted if he notices that the pup is coming to learn about scent and turn it to his advantage. Instead of tearing about aimlessly, the pup may seem to realise that on a breezy day by going to the downwind end of the cover – the end towards which the scent is carried – and by working his way back systematically he can find the dummy a great deal more easily. It is at such times that training becomes a real pleasure, and the trainer may even begin to wonder if he has a field trial champion in the making.

Working to Signals

There are many critics of the modern field trials scene. They suggest that modern trials dogs are unable to work on their own initiative and are forever looking back to the handler for instructions, rather than getting their noses down and doing the job themselves. I can only speak as one who as spectated at a few trials, and been a Gun at some more. I have seen such dogs, but I have seldom seen them among the prizes. The best retrievers are those that can be handled close to the fall of game, and then be left to their own devices by a handler who has faith in them. The great thing about handling a dog onto a given area is not to overdo it.

As I have said, a fellow Gun may ask for a bird to be picked which he has down in patch of cover. That is one thing, but in a two-acre block of cover he may add that the bird fell just behind that old stunted oak. Remembering that retrieving should be carried out at maximum efficiency in the minimum time, there is little point in leaving a dog to hunt 100 yards from this spot.

Personally, I have found that the best way to train a dog to work to hand signals, rather than letting him see the dummies being thrown, is to bring him onto an open grass area, walking at heel, where two dummies have been placed some 30 yards apart. The dog is walked up to a position directly between the dummies and sat down facing the trainer, who then takes a couple of paces backwards.

The pup is now sitting with a dummy to right and left, with the handler facing him a couple of yards away. The trainer may decide that, as the pup's attention seems to be mainly on the right-hand dummy, he will test him most by sending him for the one on the left.

The trainer now throws his left arm straight out, pointing at the dummy on that side, takes a sideways step in that direction to emphasise his arm action, and then commands 'Fetch'. If all is well, the pup will have changed its attention, and will go to pick the left-hand dummy. However, if it goes for the one on the right the stop whistle is immediately given and the signals repeated. If the pup has been able to get close to the right-hand dummy, it should be walked back at heel to its central position. Next time, the trainer will point excitedly at the right-hand dummy, walking crabwise towards it, before giving the command 'Fetch'.

This exercise requires a great deal of patience but, as in all training, once the penny has dropped with the pup it is plain sailing. In fact, when the lesson has been mastered on short grass it will be found even easier in light cover because the pup cannot see the dummy, and is more ready to accept the trainer's advice. This builds mutual confidence.

Introduction to Game

If all has gone according to plan, the pup will have reached this stage of retrieving at an age of about twelve months, at the start of September. The last formal lesson can now be completed – the introduction to game. Up until now, the pup has only retrieved dummies.

As it is September, the trainer will be able to shoot, buy, beg, borrow or steal a duck. He should look for a nice clean specimen, without blood on its plumage.

If the pup has shown any signs of sensitivity in its earlier retrieving, it may be as well to remove a sock from one of the dummies, cut off the toe to make it into a tube, and slip this over the duck so that its wings are held close, and only the neck and head and the tail are sticking out. The duck will have been shot on the previous day, giving it plenty of time to cool.

Lay the duck out, just as for a blind retrieve, and send the pup to fetch it. The second the pup puts his mouth down to pick it up, give two short peeps on the recall whistle. In nine cases out of ten the pup will hesitate for a second then pick the duck and come tearing back to the trainer with his first 'real' retrieve. If the pup hesitates for a longer time, or nibbles at the duck, the trainer goes right back to basics, calling the pup's name, blowing the recall whistle, and running away.

The next retrieve will be on warm game. The pup is taken out on the shoot, and the trainer will be praying for the chance to shoot a duck, partridge or rabbit. Pigeons are very definitely out at this early stage, because their loose breast feathers clog a pup's mouth like a bundle of cotton wool. The game is shot while the pup sits watching. The pup is left sitting while the trainer picks it up himself, to check that it is fairly clean and not bleeding profusely. Then the warm game is placed as for a blind retrieve and the pup sent to fetch it. After a few similar experiences, the pup will be ready to retrieve directly when game is shot, although the trainer will make the pup sit and wait for at least twenty seconds before sending him out, will always give wounded game a second barrel, and only allow the pup one or two retrieves out of every three to maintain steadiness.

After a month of fairly light duties on the rough shoot and beside the flight pond, the date will be well into October and soon the pup is about to face his sternest test of all. His first formal pheasant shoot is fast approaching. Other than repeating the obedience test and brushing up on any items that have slipped, all the trainer can do now is keep his fingers crossed.

12 DOGS ON THE SHOOT

Introduction to the Shoot

Any trainer who has breathed a sigh of relief at the end of the formal training sessions should think again. The dog's first season should be seen as nothing more than an extension of the training programme. That is why most trained gundogs are bought and sold after having had one season's experience in the field. The fact is that, up until then, they are still just puppies. It takes at least one season, maybe more, before a retriever will be worthy of consideration as a mature working gundog.

Equally important, the trainer must recognise that on the shoot the pup is going to be subject to a host of temptations. For one thing, he is going to be introduced to a lot of dogs that would have been better left at home – dogs that must be kept on a lead at all times and, when let off to retrieve a bird lying in the open at twenty paces, are just as likely to end up in the next county. One can't help wondering whether such brutes are brought along as nothing more than the complete package of Range Rover, flat cap, Barbour, green wellies and well manicured lady. But there we are. At least if the lady is present the dog on its lead can be handed over to her and the Gun left free to concentrate on his shooting.

Before the first formal day, the pup will have grown accustomed to gunfire in small doses. The sound of a big shoot is something very different. It is far better to build up gradually on smaller days to begin with. Of course, if the pup has been accustomed to waiting patiently in a car it may, on its first few days, be left there for the morning or afternoon. On many shoots, the bulk of the shooting is done before lunch, which may be a fairly leisurely affair, leaving just enough time for one drive or two short ones before the November daylight fades. Obviously, this provides an ideal opportunity to introduce the pup to the shoot.

Better still, though not acceptable in the case of an invited guest, is to lay the gun aside for the short afternoon and concentrate entirely on the pup. After all, on modern shoots where eight Guns shoot where six once stood the flanking Guns are often out of the action anyway. Explain to the organiser before the shoot what you are doing and why and, particularly if he is a keen dog man himself, he may be able to arrange things so that you don't miss out too much, but this should be recognised as a great favour.

Best of all is to ask around and see if it is possible to have a few day's picking up. Again, the man seeking this should explain that it is to give his first-season pup some experience or else he could find himself, with one other picker-up, responsible for cleaning up on a 300-bird day behind a team of Guns who haven't a dog between them. The wise trainer will spell it out exactly, well in advance, that all he requires is two or three retrieves and, at this stage, he will not send his dog after a runner. Obviously, this is best achieved on a friendship basis.

The First Drive

Very often the true pickers-up, men with possibly a team of retrievers, will be stationed as much as 200 yards behind the line of Guns. Their primary purpose is to pick up runners, birds which have been hit and fly on. The line of Guns

207

would probably be surprised how many birds fly on for a considerable distance, apparently unhurt, and then crumple up, stone dead.

However, if picking up at this stage is seen as nothing more than a stepping-stone on the path of having a gundog that will accompany his master while he shoots, it will be better to be up with the action. Assuming that the pup's owner has decided that the best course is to bring the pup out for the afternoon and leave his gun in the car, he should have a word with a couple of his fellow Guns and ask if they would mind some company. The reason for asking two of them is that one might be standing out in an open grass field for the drive while the other is close to some cover. In his first season, certainly for the first few shoots, the pup should never be sent to retrieve birds lying in plain view. The trainer will not want all the time and effort spent in encouraging the pup to hunt with his nose to be wasted at this stage. If this is explained to the dogless Guns, nobody will be offended when the trainer chooses to stand with the Gun closest to cover.

Having joined the Gun, the trainer will stand or sit three or four yards behind and command the pup to sit just in front of him. The majority of birds should be falling behind their position. If the pup is sitting just in front of his trainer and he falls to the temptation of a bird that falls close to them he has to pass the trainer in order to get at it, and can be grabbed by the scruff of the neck and put back into position. If this crime is committed, the pup will not be allowed a retrieve at the end of the drive. He will be made to sit and watch while the trainer picks the fallen bird himself. The trainer may think it advisable, certainly for the first few drives, to keep the pup on his lead. It is a fine sight to see a labrador sitting patiently and rock steady throughout a drive, but not to have the dog tethered takes a great deal of faith on his master's part – faith built through experience. Remember, once the shooting has started there is little time to give attention to the dog, and many owners

*For the young dog's first few visits to
the shoot, it is best that he should receive
his master's full attention.*

would rather tether a dog about whose steadiness they are not 101 per cent certain.

There is nothing worse than a loose dog running about picking up shot game willy-nilly during the course of a drive. A tether, at least, makes certain that this will never happen. It is one thing for pickers-up to have their dogs free. They can give all their attention to their dogs. Not so the man who is shooting, and particularly not when the action is fast and furious and temptation, for the dog, at its height.

Through the course of the drive, the trainer will be taking careful note of each and every bird shot by the Gun. Some will be eliminated by falling on open ground. One may be a runner, and that should be left to a more experienced dog. But, with luck, at the end of the drive the trainer will have a clear picture of the position of two or three birds that fell stone dead into light cover.

Leaving the pup sitting, the trainer will pick those birds lying in the open to reinforce the pup's steadiness. The pup will realise that he is not free to retrieve everything that flies and falls. Or maybe the Gun will volunteer to pick these birds. Anyway, the pup is then taken to a position commanding the retrieves that are for him, and sent out in the usual way. Because he has been encouraged to use his nose, and with a little judicious handling onto the area on which the pheasants fell, he should soon have completed his first retrieves.

After this, for the rest of the pup's first season, progression will be a steady matter, allowing the pup to stay out a little longer and have a few more retrieves on each day until, by mid-January, for the last days of 'cocks-only', the pup will be spending the full day at his master's side and retrieving all birds that fall into cover.

What not to retrieve

As stated, in a pup's first season, in order to encourage him to hunt with his nose, he should not be allowed to pick game lying in plain view. Equally, success after success breeds a pup's confidence in his own and his master's abilities.

Sometimes it may take the diplomacy of an archangel to avoid the request of a Gun who believes he may have a bird down 'somewhere over there', but experience shows that in ninety-nine out of a hundred of these cases the man is mistaken or simply fooling himself. Pickers-up know these characters well, and usually secrete a pheasant in the bottom of their game bags to meet such eventualities. They take a keen interest in what the Gun is telling them, probably noting that the man hasn't hit very much and is getting desperate for something to show to his fellow Guns. They then stride off purposefully, disappear for a minute or two, smoking a cigarette and having a chat with their dogs, then take the pheasant out of the bottom of their bag and stride back with it. Of course, they will have a big grin on their faces and so will everybody else when the grateful Gun mutters, 'Funny that, I could have sworn that it was a hen bird.'

The point is that if you put a young dog onto a doubtful bird, after he has been searching for five or ten minutes he will be thoroughly frustrated, up goes his head, and he is no longer using his nose.

Also with runners, it is one thing to send a fairly inexperienced dog after a pheasant which is very obviously on its last legs but quite another to send it after a wingtipped cock which can run like the wind. Equally, a cock pheasant may decide to fight it out with beak and spur rather than come quietly. Again, this can wreck the confidence of a pup in his first season. Far better to leave it to a more experienced dog. Incidentally, even an old campaigner should not be sent to retrieve until the runner has disappeared from sight for a minute or so. Given time, the pheasant may squat; but if it sees a labrador hot on its heels it will probably keep on running like an express train. Also, if the bird is running in the open it encourages the dog to hunt with his eyes. A gundog should hunt like a foxhound rather than a greyhound – even if there are some that might be considered for entry in the Waterloo Cup, the greatest prize in hare coursing, whenever fur is up and running.

End of the Season

It should be obvious that a dog is not like a gun. The dog cannot simply be put away at the end of the shooting season to be taken out eight months later, dusted down and expected to perform perfectly. A gun requires maintenance and servicing. A dog needs something more.

One of the problems is that for those who have heavy work and family commitments to meet it is all too tempting to think that there is no need to give the gundog any more than the bare minimum of attention through the closed season. Its working role over, the dog reverts to being a family pet, pure and simple. It sees its master at meal times, and maybe they have a fairly long walk on Sundays. In fact, just one decent walk a week can be enough to keep a gundog's performance ticking over so that come the next season it just needs a slight rise in tempo to get back into the swing of things, rather than having to start from scratch.

It is obedience training, far more than work associated purely with working to the gun, that needs the closest attention. The small test of obedience described in the previous chapter, if done on a fortnightly basis, acts as a refresher as well as highlighting anything that may be going wrong. For example, if the dog is regularly taken for walks by someone other than the trainer and master he or she may not understand why the dog should always be kept at heel. In fact, the dog may never be at heel except when he is on a lead. Naturally, it is far more fun for the dog to be allowed to 'do his own thing' and it won't be long before he is showing a marked reluctance not to stray off all the time. Many owners themselves let standards slip in this respect. It does seem hard on the dog not to let him run about.

The best solution when going for a walk is to keep the dog at heel for half of the time, and let him run about for the rest. Of course, in some labradors the instinct to stay to heel is so strong that they simply do not want to gallop about.

Whether or not to give dummy retrieves during the closed season months is a matter to be approached with some caution. Certainly there are dogs who, after experience of the real thing, will show little interest in an old sock. Probably one retrieve a week is sufficient, and it should always be made interesting to keep the dog fresh. For example, my labradors are keen swimmers and we have a small river about fifty yards from our house. Rather than simply getting them to sit and watch while I throw a dummy into the water, I may throw a dummy clean over the river and into cover well behind the opposite bank. Others will have their own situations and solutions, and plan accordingly.

At the end of the day, training and working a retriever, or any gundog, is to steer a path between letting the dog please himself and maybe run riot at one extreme and at the other to nag away at the dog until all his natural drive, pace, style and game-finding ability are lost. As the last word on this particular subject, whether a man trains and handles his own pup or buys a ready-trained dog, he will find after a few months that what he has is little more or less than he deserves.

13   FINALE

Winter daylight fades fast towards the monochrome of dusk. The last drive of the day's shooting ended half an hour ago. There is just enough time for the pheasants to return to the home woods. Flurry of wings and chortling calls echo as the birds fly up to their sheltered perches in spruce and pine. If they roosted on the ground, pheasants would fall easy prey to marauding foxes.

In the big house, the Guns and their guests are sitting down to tea. It will not be long before they are homeward bound. It was not always so. In the days when travel was not so easy, the majority of them would be staying at least for one night. Their valets, who had possibly spent the day loading when their masters shot with pairs of guns, would have run baths and laid out clothes before retiring to the servant's hall to eat their meal and perhaps flirt with the resident maids. Dinner upstairs would have been a sumptuous affair. On some of the great estates, following a big shoot, a ball would be held and the roads for miles around would ring to the sharp hoofbeats of horses pulling carriages. During the reigns of Edward VII and George V, who served to raise shooting to the pinnacle of society's activities, who had shot what, where and when was reported in many of the national newspapers. All this has changed. Indeed the wind of change that put an end to so many aspects of British life tore like a gale through the carefully tended coverts of the traditional shooting scene.

As tea is finished, and the whisky decanter comes out for a last, farewell drink, some of the older Guns may recall such days. Perhaps they will hanker for the old life style.

This is not the place to write or comment on the social history of Britain during the last century, and how it has affected the fortunes of the countryside and landed families. However, I dare say that historians will chronicle a redistribution of wealth out of the pockets of a minority into the hands of a majority. For driven game shooting, once held as the preserve of the rich and noble, the effects have been radical.

At the most obvious extreme of the spectrum, great estates where owners entertained friends, relations and social desirables on the grandest of scales are now forced to consider the sporting potential of their ground as a financial rather than social asset. Where the owner is a keen shooting man, he may keep a day or two for himself and personal guests but the rest will be let for as high a price as his agent can squeeze from the market.

Today, when those involved in the management and marketing of pheasant shooting take a 'busman's holiday' with guns in their hands, much of the conversation at lunch and tea is concerned with the harsh financial realities of who is getting what, and at what price. On one thing they are all agreed, and it is something that gives hope for the future. Shooting men of experience are no longer prepared to pay for poor-quality pheasants and, what is more, they are prepared to pay a large premium for outstanding birds. This is ably demonstrated by prices sought for pheasant shooting for the season into 1990. Prices range from as little or less than £12 per bird shot to prices of twice that figure or more. Top prices are paid for the highest, most testing pheasants enjoyed in the right setting and without any stinting on the facilities offered, down to the last mouthful of smoked salmon and drop of champagne. And believe me, as one who is involved in the management and letting of shooting, it is the best days, achieving the highest prices, which sell themselves and for which there is no lack of the right sort of customer.

As tea draws to a close in the house, and the Guns exchange brief confidential mutterings to ensure their tip should be neither too large nor too small, beaters and pickers-up are enjoying their chatter in the shed behind the keeper's cottage. The host is a generous man who provides them with a bottle of whisky and some cans of beer. Those who have to drive home may be slipping their cans unopened into their jacket pockets. They make do with the last dregs of tea from their lunchtime flasks. The soft buzz of contented conversation is broken by guffaws of laughter as the local comics offer their own interpretation of the day's events, with nobody spared from their ribald humour. In more serious moments, some of the beaters may be discussing their own shoots. Many beaters are self-employed tradesmen who give up a day to help out on the shoot for the company and from their sheer love of the sport. The ten pound note in their pocket at the end of the day means little to them; they could have earned it in an hour. And, for some of them, much of their time is given over to running their own self-help shoots of either driven shooting on a smaller scale or top-quality rough shooting. These smaller shoots are the backbone of game shooting.

Later still, the old stop is back at his cottage. While he waits for his meal, he sits at his fireside, sucking meditatively on his pipe, and absent-mindedly strokes the ears of the little terrier curled up on his lap.

As he mulls over the events of the day, he thinks how well the drive from Long Wood has turned out since the boss gave Bert, the keeper, the go-ahead to cut out a new flushing ride. Then he thinks of that daft young boy of George's who never keeps his place in the line, and is forever shouting and hallooing when he should hold his tongue and tap his stick. Then there was that fool of a dog with one of the Guns which nearly ruined the second drive after lunch, running about in the middle of the drive, picking up birds here and dropping them there. It took off after a runner, dashing into Home Wood where the birds had been gathering throughout the day. Fool dog, he thought, but more fool the man who had brought such an untrained wild beast along with him.

'Did you have a good day?' his wife calls from the kitchen. His mind runs back to that first drive where he watched the birds soaring high out over the valley before sidling off with a drop and a curl. Too stiff a test for some of the Guns. He thinks of the nice young man with the pretty wife who stopped for a few words and to offer him a pull from his flask. He thinks of the happy chatter of his friends. And he thinks of the conversation between the driver of the game cart, the young picker-up and himself. He takes his pipe from his mouth.

'Don't know many shooting days that ain't, my dear. No, I don't know many days that ain't. Yes, we had a right good day,' he replies.

And his wife, like many another good woman married to a man with shooting in his bones, simply shrugs and smiles.